THE RIGHT WAY TO
KEEP PET FISH

By
REGINALD DUTTA
B.A., F.Z.S., OF FISH TANKS, LTD.

With a Foreword by
H. F. VINALL
FORMERLY CURATOR, LONDON ZOO AQUARIUM

Fish drawings (Breeds) by
L. R. BRIGHTWELL, F.Z.S., F.R.H.S.

GRAMERCY PUBLISHING COMPANY · NEW YORK

ABOUT THE AUTHOR

His designs of tanks, his original treatment of their interior decor, his pioneer use of new materials, have all long been trend-setters. His fame as a 'fish doctor' has helped to establish an international reputation – amongst the Royalty of four nations, the distinguished and the famous in industry, entertainment, and the academics.

As the Managing Director of London's oldest established fish specialists his up-to-date advice will prove invaluable – unique in fact.

AN IMPORTANT NOTE

The reader should be aware of the use of Centigrade as a measuring system for temperature in this book. For instance, 23° Centigrade equals approximately 73° Fahrenheit. To convert Centigrade to Fahrenheit, multiply by 9, divide by 5 and add 32°.

Following is a simple conversion table for other measuring systems used in this book:

Centimeter (Cm.) = 0.3937 in.
Meter = 3.2808 feet
Cubic Centimeter (Cu. Cm. or CC.) = 0.0610 Cu. In.
Liter = 0.2642 Gal.
Gram = 0.0353 Oz.
Gram = 64.799 milligrams

Foreword

I AM asked to read many books on fish. A large proportion of them are of too technical a nature for the amateur aquarist – who has only a limited amount of time to devote to his hobby – to understand.

Mr. Dutta's book is different and I am therefore happy to recommend this excellent and clearly written piece of work. He knows his subject and has devoted himself to the task of producing a most informative and instructive volume. It should be invaluable to those who have taken up (or are about to take up) the ever-increasing art of fish-keeping. It is an absorbing hobby and, to its many devotees, a source of delight.

Those who aim at success could not do better than to read and digest this book. With its concise style, it is a splendid addition to those already published and should fulfil a real need. I wish it every success.

H. F. VINALL,
Curator,
London Zoo Aquarium.

Contents

1
True Meaning of Quality

WHY IT IS EASY TO CHEAT A CUSTOMER

THE trouble with specialized trades like furs, jewels, or tropical fish, is that it is so very easy to cheat the people who have not sufficient knowledge of the subject to protect themselves from unscrupulousness. Methods of 'price clipping' are many and varied, but the following will illustrate the sort of difficulty confronting the customer:

A later chapter describes how to breed good, healthy fish, but there are two important points on which everything depends: firstly, that too many baby fish should not be put in one tank so that they become overcrowded and, through want of sufficient oxygen, food and space, degenerate into poor specimens; second, the temperature of the breeding tank should not be kept so high as to cause the fish to grow at an unnatural pace. Under such overcrowding and temperatures the fish become 'forced-bred'. That is to say, when as babies they are kept at higher than normal temperatures, packed into a tank in greater numbers than safety rules allow, often being given strong aeration by pumping air bubbles into their water, then they very quickly grow to saleable size. Such fish can be sold at much lower prices than those reared properly, but they have two very serious disadvantages. They are constitutionally weak and, although not actually sick at the time of sale, are far more liable to disease. They practically never mature into fine specimens in size, shape or colour. Only an expert can detect such frauds – which is what these forced-bred fish are – and almost the sole protection for the public is the reputation of the dealer and their belief in his technical ability.

The dealer is assumed to be a *specialist*. A general knowledge on his part of all forms of pets such as dogs, cats, birds, and so forth, is no more satisfactory than is an average knowledge of clothes in judging furs. The aquarist should have a specialized training because his subject is so new and rapidly expanding with many new varieties of fish. The latest research, books, or experts to whom he can turn for information are all so scarce that he cannot hope to give the customer satisfactory service if his energies are dissipated over 'pets' as a whole.

As will be repeatedly shown in this book, the pond or aquarium can be free of trouble *provided* there is specialist knowledge available somewhere along the line; if the customer does not have it, then his dealer simply must fill the gap.

This matter of the customer–dealer relationship is so important that no excuse is made for stressing it. The example given of the forced-bred fish is intended merely as an illustration, and does not exhaust the methods of cutting prices, methods which the customer is unable to prove or even to see. Fortunately there are a number of ways of helping the customer to form an opinion of the dealer, and the more important are listed below:

FORMING AN OPINION OF THE DEALER

1. *Tanks displaying fish for sale should always be of large size*
This is a vital point, the full significance of which is not always understood. In later chapters the principle of the 'balanced tank', showing how many fish can be kept in it, will be explained, but the point now is that the tanks should be big enough. In a large aquarium the fish may seem few in number, it may appear that the dealer is not offering a good assortment from which to choose; BUT the fish will be healthy – that is what matters.

From the dealer's point of view, the small tank lowers his overhead costs, makes it easier and quicker to catch fish, and gives a better 'display' when lots of fish are jammed together instead of being scattered in large volumes of water. But the customer suffers as fish kept in such conditions are bound to be weakened and to fall sick unless removed quickly.

2. *Fish should be isolated before sale*
Isolation of fish before their sale to the public is a service the good dealer will always give. This is because fish may carry

disease, or be sick themselves, so that quarantine of a few days is the only real safeguard. If the fish have been obtained from new or untried sources, for example importations from abroad, a much longer period of separation is required.

The point about isolation is the degree to which it really is carried out; lip-service is one thing, regular and conscientious attention another.

Pressure by the customer who wants 'something cheap' and who compares fish solely/mainly on price has made this service very difficult to maintain, but a few stalwarts still do so. The alternative is to shift the burden on to the (get-it-cheaper) customer and to let him have a quarantine tank of his own for new purchases.

3. *General thoroughness*
Apart from the obvious point of having clean tanks, the good dealer will go to the trouble to equalize water temperatures before taking the fish out of one tank to put into another. This point may seem small, but the experienced customer knows its importance, as will be seen by a study of the later chapter on diseases and their causes. There should not be a difference greater than 1 degree C., when fish are being moved from one water to another.

Here again there is all the difference between lip service and not bothering when no customer is looking.

4. *Thoughtfulness*
How many catching nets does the dealer use? Beware the man who has only one – so that disease can be transferred from display tank to display tank.

Does the dealer always use the same jar or other container, into which he puts the fish before transferring them to the plastic bag you take home – complete with every disease in the shop.

Does he have warmed wrapping up materials handy?

Does he love and know his fish? Or does he scoop up a squirming mass of suffocating/distressed/crushed helpless creatures and then leisurely pick one out by hand? The body temperature for fish is cold; touching it by hand (nearly 38°C.) is like taking a red-hot poker to it.

9

Does he feed his own stock regularly? And with varied foods?

Many are the signs that give away a thoughtless – and, therefore, unsatisfactory – dealer!

Conclusion

The moral of this chapter is that the dealer *must be a specialist* who knows his job, and he must be conscientious and not indulge in price reduction at the expense of quality.

The 'man in the pet shop' did a great service in introducing the hobby to the public, but the march of events has now made his position extremely difficult, as the goldfish-in-a-bowl is as obsolete as the crystal set. Modern, scientifically-balanced aquaria require specialist knowledge constantly kept up to date.

2
A Community Aquarium

IN a modern aquarium the water need never be changed. Never!

WHY THE WATER NEED NEVER BE CHANGED

Fish consume oxygen dissolved in the water and give off harmful carbon-dioxide gases. All that is necessary is to provide the oxygen supply and to get rid of the gases, and this can be done in four ways:

1. Sufficiently large air surface of the water, so that the fresh oxygen is taken in and the bad gases escape at a fast enough rate. This is the greatest single factor of success.
2. Relative to the size of the air surface, i.e. the area of water in actual contact with the atmosphere, there should not be too many or too big fish, otherwise the oxygen is consumed and the bad gases are produced too fast.
3. Growing plants to break down the carbon dioxide gases and to turn them into oxygen and into nitrates; the oxygen helps the fish and the nitrates act as fertilizers for the plants themselves. These plants are known as 'oxygenators'.
4. Light to make the plants grow.

The balanced tank is thus quite easily obtainable. Naturally there should be no excess dirt, especially in the way of uneaten food. Nor need we concern ourselves with the purists who maintain that after several *years* the chemical contents of the water increase to the detriment of the fish. The normal usages of siphoning off some water and of replacing evaporation largely discount this objection.

Excess dirt, and excess urine which gives ammonia distress to the fish gill plates, are the chief points of danger to watch for. Your filter (has it been cleaned recently?) should cope with this – if it's big enough! – otherwise you ought to siphon off

30 per cent to 40 per cent of the water from the tank base and top up with clean warmed water, to replace the tank water thus removed.

Modern power filters are now so good that there should be no problem.

HOW DEEP SHOULD THE TANK BE?

It should be noted that the depth of a tank adds little to its fish capacity, as the vital factor is the opening to the air, that is the length and the width from back to front. In fact, excess depth from top to bottom is harmful in that a difference in temperature is caused, since the hotter water rises to the top and the colder water sinks to the bottom. Plants grown in too deep a tank tend to straggle. An irritating number of things seem to 'go wrong' with these deep tanks, the reasons not being always apparent – extra water pressure or failure of light to penetrate down are only partial explanations – but explained or not, deep tanks result in trouble.

This desire for great depth is a common mistake made by the layman, particularly the architect or the interior decorator, and is another illustration why the specialized dealer should be used for guidance; by doing so, a trouble-free aquarium is obtained which will be beautiful and a thing of joy.

If you have a deep tank, then please do have adequate power filtration. Modern techniques of bonding glass to glass are encouraging increased depths, and genuinely strong enough aerators are needed to take the strain.

So long as the water surface is large, there is no harm in using glass covers or close-fitting toplights; even if these were almost airtight there would be enough oxygen in a cushion of air 1 or 2 cm. thick, trapped between the top of the water and the glass cover, to contain enough oxygen for a good many hours; nor should the carbon dioxide concentration become harmful in that period. During this time the cover should normally be displaced, even momentarily, for feeding, etc., thus renewing the oxygen supply of this air cushion and letting out the used-up 'bad' air.

HOW MANY FISH IN A TANK?

The following are guiding principles for the number of fish in a community tank; but in case of doubt a specialist should be consulted. Filters increase this capacity by 40 per cent, power filters by 100 per cent.

Number of tropical fish, average body length 3cm.	Area of tank water surface	Suggested depth of tank, top to bottom
18	45cm. × 30cm.	30cm. × 38cm.
24–28	60cm. × 30cm.	30cm. × 45cm.
36–40	90cm. × 30cm.	30cm. × 50cm.
48–55	120cm. × 30cm.	30cm. × 60cm.

Coldwater fish. Usually these are much larger than Tropicals and one body cm. of fish, measured lengthways, is calculated to consume the oxygen absorbed by 365 square centimetres of water surface (same as the number of days in a year). Hence very few, and very small, coldwater fish can be kept in an aquarium; goldfish, rudd, orfe, carp, etc., are *not* suitable and they are better in outdoor ponds. The cruelty of keeping goldfish in a bowl is clear. The air surface of the bowl is too small to supply oxygen for a fast-moving, quick-growing type like a goldfish, even if it lingers on in its uncomfortably cramped prison for a few years, stunted in growth and suffering in slow suffocation. A goldfish should normally live a quarter of a century in the more natural environment of a pond, and grow to its full length of over 35cm. For a coldwater aquarium, then, we suggest slow-moving fish that do not grow too fast, for example shubunkins, fantails, telescopic-eyed moors, veiltails, lionheads, orandas, but *not* goldfish!

The above are safe capacity guides, allowing for such factors as increased heat causing the water to have a lower oxygen content, or for excess dirt causing a limited amount of fouling. The suggested number of fish can be exceeded, particularly by the addition of aeration, and, if you do have more fish, it is recommended. So beware of buying new fish from tanks crowded beyond these limits, or of overcrowding your own.

DANGERS

Shells, ornaments and rocks can most certainly be used in a community aquarium, but only with great care as a dangerously high proportion are harmful to fish.

Many kinds of rocks, in particular, slowly dissolve in water, resulting in an imperceptible but definite clouding of the water and, much more important, this dissolution alters the chemical content of the water with results that are harmful to fish even to the point of death. Yet rocks add greatly to the beauty of the aquascape, and several guaranteed harmless types are now sold and their use is enjoyed by thousands of aquarists. Your dealer must guide you in this matter.

An important point to remember is that within reason it is not the volume of water which counts but the area in contact with the air. Thus if a tank is lavishly decorated with sand and aquatic rocks, giving a beautiful effect but displacing some of the water, there is no harm done because the air surface has not been reduced. Piling the sand in hills and dales so that the fish have varying depths of water to choose from is helpful to their health, in addition to being decorative.

Technical knowledge is also vital in the case of the sand used at the bottom of the aquarium. If too fine it will seem to 'matt' down and choke the plants; if too coarse it tends to trap greater amounts of food and excreta and so cause fouling. It is also true that fish like to pick up mouthfuls of sand, 'chewing it over' and keeping the nourishing particles mixed therein and spitting out the rest. Thus sand must be suitable for this purpose.

PLANTS AND LIGHT

Soil, loam, etc., are unnecessary for the ordinary growth of plants in a community aquarium; it is another matter propagating plants on a commercial scale or growing extra fine specimens where the fish are a secondary consideration.

Light is necessary for the health of the plants to enable them to absorb the carbon-dioxide gases the fish breathe out. Too much light will cause the appearance of microscopic life known

14

as algae, and cause the water to turn green; insufficient light kills the plants.

In general, the aquarium in a bright room should have about four hours artificial light; in a dark room up to eight or even ten hours daily. The strength of the artificial light should be approximately 25 watts per square foot of water surface, and the electric bulbs should be within 10cm. of the water. There is no particular point in using coloured, fluorescent or strip-lighting, but equally there is no particular objection, provided the light is properly diffused over the whole surface so that all the plants have a fair share and grow. Concentration of light in one spot, leaving the rest of the tank in semi-darkness, ruins the oxygenating plants and causes all sorts of trouble. The worst type of toplight is a small piece of bent metal, just large enough to shield an electric bulb, resting on a piece of glass; this is often sold because it is cheap, although its 'cheapness' becomes problematical after frequent replacement of plants.

An aquarium is better situated in a dark spot where the amount of light it receives can be exactly controlled by using electric bulbs, instead of relying on the whims of daylight. By contrast, too, the internal aquarium lighting shows up better in a dark corner.

'Glo-lux' type of lighting that eliminates the 'yellow caste' in water and which highlights the colours of the fish, especially the blues, reds and greens, has become deservedly popular.

Many people also like 'speciality lighting'. Secondary illumination, perhaps shining 'from afar' or through the water (as distinct from above), gives a soft, muted effect, soothing and relaxing to the onlooker.

Alternatively, for the hearty, extrovert, gay, cocktail bar, three phase lighting is available. This switches rhythmically from bright-all-over (perhaps in varied colours) to a single-intensely-focused-beam playing on a special motif, (which might be waving plants swaying in aeration bubbles, or a lovely coloured rock/coral/ornament) and finished with a dramatic pause of darkness – before the tank reappears in bright light as the phase re-starts its cycle.

CONCLUSION

If the above points seem complicated, it should be remembered that a specialized dealer would take care of them automatically, and the customer's co-operation would be limited in practice to switching the electric light on for the required number of hours. If no specialized knowledge is available trouble is encountered unnecessarily. These remarks apply to all aquaria, whether coldwater or tropical.

These points are further discussed in *Tropical Fish and Fish Tanks*, *Tropical Fish* (Octopus Books) and in *Tropical Fish Owner's Encyclopedia*, all by the same author. Also the *Pelham Manual for Fish Tank Owners*. Thanks are due to Elliot Right Way Books for allowing mention of these books by other Publishers.

3

Setting Up the Tank, and General Maintenance; Coldwater or Tropical

SETTING UP THE TANK

THE first thing to decide is its situation. A place where the aquarium is subject to wide fluctuations in room temperature is not the best – for example, right by an outside window where the outside air might change from hot to cold, throwing unnecessary strain on the internal heating elements of the tank; in this case the back of the aquarium should be separated from the window glass by some form of insulation such as a sheet of cardboard, plywood, felt, etc. Excess light from the window can turn the water green, as explained in Chapter 5, unless shading is provided.

Instructions on installing the aquarium are usually supplied at the time of sale, but the following, listed in order of operation, may prove of interest:

1. The sand to be used should be thoroughly washed. This must be done most painstakingly, as dirt left in it will later cloud the tank. It is easier to wash sand in small doses. The inside of the aquarium could be cleaned first and the newly washed sand then introduced bit by bit as it is ready; otherwise water from the washed sand would seep all over the place.

   Incidentally, never clean the outside of the aquarium unless this is full, otherwise the pressure applied when wiping the glass falls wholly on the putty, and there is a strong likelihood that this will be dislodged (slightly) and so cause the tank to leak. When the tank is full, however, there is considerable internal water pressure to hold the glass firmly in position, and the outside of the tank can then be safely polished.

17

2. In the case of the Tropical tank, the heater and thermostat should be fitted. There are so many types of these now available that directions for fitting your particular one should be obtained at the time of purchase.

3. The sand and the guaranteed harmless rocks should be arranged to suit your artistic taste, but the heater should be kept right down at the lowest point of the tank since heat rises; if the sand is arranged in hills and dales, the heater ought to be laid horizontally in a dale. Care should be taken, however, not to bury the heater in the sand.

   Heaped-up sand should be anchored by rocks, otherwise it will flatten out when water is poured in. Sometimes the sand is arranged to slope down to the front; in this way sediment and droppings from the fish tend to accumulate there and are more easily siphoned off, as explained below. Incidentally, the thermostat must also be kept clear of the sand or it will give false readings.

4. The tank should be filled gently, very gently. A plate held at sand level will break the fall of the water and will therefore prevent the sand churning up and clouding the tank – often for days. Once the tank has been filled it should not be moved, otherwise the internal water pressure will cause leaks.

5. The correct amount of greenery needed to balance the tank should be planted; usually it is preferred to group in bunches, but these should not be too thick or inserted too deeply into the sand. In the case of large tanks, planting can better be done when only half full of water. The plants with roots should have covering only as far as their 'crown' – that is, so that the white part is buried but not the green; cuttings should be inserted up to 1½ cms. *It is important that all plants be kept wet while these operations are being carried out*, otherwise they will later tend to shrivel and dry in the aquarium – sometimes very quickly – at the least their growth will be seriously retarded. A judicious combination of plant thickets and 'caves' formed by the rocks will provide hiding-places for fish if they are off colour.

6. The toplight, usually supplied with the aquarium, should be connected and plugged in.

7. To adjust the thermostat, three things should be remembered:

A. The water takes a long time to change temperature (from one to four hours) so that an adjustment of the control knob of the thermostat does not show a reading on the thermometer for some time.

B. *Very slight* adjustments of the control knob of the thermostat are all that are required, otherwise this delicate instrument will be spoilt. Perhaps one-eighth, one-quarter, or at most half a turn will suffice. Once the thermostat has been set at the required temperature further adjustments should be unnecessary, as this temperature will be automatically maintained.

C. Water should never be allowed to wet the top mechanism of the thermostat unless it is a submersible type.

All is now ready. In all cases it is advisable to wait five days, or even a week, to allow the plants to grow and the water to get 'old', before introducing the fish. Water that has been standing for some time under the action of light becomes 'old', that is, has microscopic life born into it – a fact greatly appreciated by the fish.

GENERAL MAINTENANCE

The general maintenance of an aquarium is virtually nil. The two golden rules are not to overfeed and not to overcrowd. From time to time the tank water will evaporate and should be replaced gently, with water of the *same temperature*, simply because a water-line that shows spoils the decorative effect. Once a week, or two weeks, the inside of the aquarium glass can be wiped slowly, to clean it. Either a small scraper bought for the purpose will do, or a clean handkerchief-sized cloth – the smallest and cleanest duster will prove too large and will almost certainly leave annoying pieces of fluff in the water.

Skim the top of the aquarium water frequently especially if the smell of paint or varnish has done harm. However, this can be done in the same way the housewife skims excess fat off soup, by drawing a sheet of paper placed flat along the top of the water and dragged from one side to the other; the oil or grease will cling to the paper and so be removed.

SIPHONING

With proper care and no overfeeding there should be negligible amounts of sediment to remove, and this should be done say, once a month. Many 'automatic' types of siphon are available and are probably better suited to the average hobbyist. Some, however, prefer to use a bucket and a siphon tube – that is, a piece of rubber tubing about two metres long with an approximate diameter of one cm.; by completely filling this tube with water, from the tap, sealing both ends with the thumbs, and releasing both ends simultaneously (with the aquarium end of the tube under water) the water from the aquarium will flow down into a bucket placed on the floor, and as it flows it will carry the dirt with it. Care should be taken not to siphon out a fish by mistake – something that can happen much more easily than is imagined – and it helps to hold the aquarium end of the siphon tube not more than a fraction above the sand (and sediment) level. No harm is done if some sand is siphoned off too. Usually about the bottom 30 per cent of water is removed in this process. The aim is to remove as much sediment and as little water as possible. After a little practice this will be seen to be quite easy.

When the work is finished the aquarium should be topped up with water of the *same* temperature.

INTRODUCING NEW FISH

When a few new fish are being introduced it is a good plan to feed those already established in the tank extra well, on this one occasion only, and while they are busy eating at one end gently to tip in the newcomers at the other. The new arrivals are thus given a chance to settle down, to find hiding-places, and generally to take stock of the situation before meeting the crowd, as it were. Of course, the water temperatures will have been equalized before the transfer; to do this, the bag containing the fish can be hung, or floated, in the aquarium until its water temperature becomes the same as that of the tank, usually in 15–30 minutes. Dirty cans should be carefully wiped before being floated. Once the temperatures have been equalized, the can may be gently tipped, allowing its water to flow out and the fish to swim straight into the aquarium without being netted or handled.

BULLY FISH

Fish that are too boisterous and are inclined to throw their weight about can be 'stood in the corner' by being imprisoned in a large jam-jar. The water for the jar must be taken from the aquarium to ensure that there is no temperature change. If the jar is only two-thirds full it will float safely in the aquarium and maintain its temperature. The top should be covered lest the fish get frightened and try to jump out; it could be released after 12–24 hours. No smell in the jar please, of jam, pickles, tobacco, etc.

CATCHING FISH

Rather than chase the elusive creature all round the tank and ruin the plants and general appearance in the process, it is easier to chase the fish *into* the net.

Holding the net in a good position so that it can quickly be pulled upwards, not forwards because the fish will prove too quick for that, a ruler or another small net can be used to drive the fish into the main net.

TEMPERATURE

The temperature range of most aquaria of tropical fish is fairly wide, 18°C. to 29°C., with extreme ranges down to 7°C. and up to 35°C.; but a community tank should normally be kept *between* 22°C. and 27°C. Lest the above remark regarding the extreme temperature range be misunderstood, tropical fish in water colder than 20°C. will soon die unless heated up within a few hours, but they can perfectly well undertake a 12–18 hours journey by land, sea or air, entailing a marked temperature drop. Provided the water cools *gradually*, fish do not often suffer harm. This factor makes a journey possible and electricity failures or power cuts not nearly so frightening as some people think.

If emergency measures are needed to keep the fish water warm, a good plan is to fill a bottle with hot water and immerse this in the aquarium; it is thus possible to retain sufficient heat all night, especially if a covering rug over the whole aquarium is used as well. The introduction of hot water straight into the tank is not advisable as there is a danger of cracking the aquarium glass.

SIGNS OF TROUBLE

The hobbyist will soon sense if anything is going wrong with the tank. The first sign of the fish being unwell is that the dorsal fin folds up; this fin on top of the back should be erect. Another sign is when fish go off their food, or keep unusually still, for example at the same corner of the tank – be it at the top or bottom. In such cases, Chapter 5 should be consulted and if this does not provide sufficient guidance the help of the specialist dealer should be enlisted as soon as possible. He will need to be told as much relevant 'case history' as is practicable – whether there are any particular symptoms, any recent purchases, any points of Chapter 5 applicable. He may require to be shown samples of the aquarium sand and water. Any dead fish, *freshly* preserved in water or in pure alcohol should also be taken to him for examination.

The whole chapter applies to both tropical and to coldwater aquaria.

4
Feeding

THERE are two main foods – live and prepared.
The live are better, but they are difficult to obtain in constant, all-the-year-round supply. Fish will thrive quite well on a mixture of live and prepared foods; in fact they can get along without any live food if that proves necessary.

AMOUNT

The golden rule about feeding is simple: *Do not overfeed:* All the food given, *including* that which falls to the bottom of the pond or aquarium, should be completely eaten in about three minutes. For example, twelve tropical fish of ordinary size (body measurement about 3cm. long) or three coldwater aquaria fish of, say 5cm. body measurement, should be given

enough prepared food only to cover this circle:

that is, about one quarter of one pinch – and that is enough. The whole amount (including that at the bottom of the tank) must be eaten very quickly. The frequency of feeding is a matter of some controversy, but once or twice a day should be sufficient. Tropical fish at 21°C. or below, are sluggish and eat little; at 24°C. they are ravenous; at 28°C. and above, the lowered oxygen content of the water again robs them of their appetite. Similarly with coldwater fish; at say, 13°C., 18°C. and 22°C.; the only point is that coldwater fish vary so much in their temperature tolerance that these figures are very, very approximate.

The ideal temperatures are, then, for tropical fish: 23°C. to 26°C., and for non-tropical: 16°C. to 19°C.

As is now well known, fish can go for long periods without any food whatsoever, so that if the owner plans to be away for

23

a week he need make no special provision for the long-established community tank; the microscopic life already present in the water will be sufficient for that period of time. This course is strongly recommended in preference to allowing an unskilled stranger to feed the fish; a stranger might be tempted to be mistakenly generous with unfortunate results – after all, one pinch a day is four times too much, and spread over a week could dirty a tank. If a stranger *must* be trusted with the feeding, a good idea is to make up tiny packets for him, each sufficient for one day's meal, which he will use and not have to rely on his own judgement. The owner could profitably feed up the fish on live food for ten days or so prior to departure so as to store up surplus fat energy in the fish, on which they can draw in his absence. BUT all traces of excess excreta or uneaten food must be siphoned off before departure lest the water be fouled.

Special 'vacation' blocks that dissolve slowly in water to release predetermined amounts of food are an excellent substitute and so are the new 'jelly-type' foods that dissolve very slowly, so that the fish can eat them over a period of days, while you are away.

TYPES OF PREPARED FOODS

The choice is almost limitless; every country seems to market its own brands and there is no excuse for a monotonous diet – fish need variety as much as we do.

The old granular, or crumb type, foods have largely been displaced by flakes, manufactured under strict laboratory conditions. Sometimes these offer single ingredients (shrimp, meal, liver, beef, etc.), sometimes they are mixed with vitamins, sometimes they are in the form of multi-flake conglomerates, and sometimes you find them packed in 'menu' form where each tin of food has different compartments so that particular ingredients can be varied at will.

The 'freeze-dried' revolution has added a new dimension: just as we can get frozen fruits out of season, so too can fish now get vitamin fresh freeze-dried delicacies.

Then there are 'jelly-type' foods that are almost insoluble in water, hence do not foul it, and which can be left in the tank for previously unheard of periods.

Please do not forget that many fish are vegetarians by preference and rather resent lumps of meat-compounds being flung at them; the answer is to make sure they have adequate 'green-stuff' mixture foods, of which plenty are available.

If in desperation fish are reduced to eating the tank plants, do not blame them. It's your fault. Is the diet too monotonous? too lop-sided? How many different brands? How much live foods? (see below).

LIVE FOODS

The very best of foods are live insects and worms, and these can usually be obtained from a specialist dealer.

Daphnia is the favourite, universally acknowledged as such. Red tubifex worms, white enchytrae worms, brine shrimp, bloodworms and earthworms, are also beneficial. The trouble with gathering these foods from rivers, duckponds and other natural sources, is the very real danger of introducing water enemies and diseases, described in later chapters, and the hobbyist should be extremely wary on these points; expert screening is essential before use. Special foods for breeding are also dealt with later.

Should live foods not be available, a satisfactory substitute is to hang into the tank, on a cotton thread, a tiny piece of meat (preferably white), fish, liver, shrimp, prawn, roe, lettuce, boiled spinach, etc., in fact almost anything edible that does not dissolve in water; for example, corned beef contains a high percentage of fat, which will dirty the water, and should not, therefore, be used. The substitute can be cooked or raw, but thoroughly washed so as to avoid fouling the water; for instance, the blood from raw meat should have been washed out first. One morsel 3cm. long by 3cm. thick ought to suffice for twelve standard fish (body measurement 3cm.) and should be left in the tank for 30–40 minutes at a time. Again, frequency of feeding is a matter of controversy, but once or twice a day should be ample. If possible, a new substitute should be used each time. Two or three pieces could be hung, at different heights, so as to allow the shy and the weak to feed more easily.

FOOTNOTES

Different kinds of food produce different results. An exclusive diet of oatmeal and of chopped-up white worms is fattening and is sometimes used, as in the case of the veiltails, to produce fish with short, rounded bodies, heavy and even a little clumsy. On the other hand, dry prepared foods of the flake type, and the slightly laxative live Daphnia, tend to produce normal fast-swimming fish.

Red tubifex worms will stay alive for days in a jam-jar standing under a slow-running tap; the *continuous* flow of water washes away any dead worms leaving the nice bright red ones in a tight cluster at the bottom of the jar.

Live Daphnia is usually sold in plastic bags, containing water and pure oxygen and food for the daphnia, so that these stay alive and fresh for several days – you can now buy a week's supply at only one trip to the shop.

5

Things That Go Wrong
Coldwater and Tropical

ALL living creatures, whether human or fish, can fall sick. Curing them requires knowledge which the layman cannot hope to acquire without years of study and experience – in other words, without becoming a specialist himself. Therefore he should rely, and rightly so, on his dealer.

As with human diseases, the doctor is called only for the more serious cases, and there are many things the layman can learn so as to be able to recognize signs of danger and to apply the more simple remedies.

CLOUDY WATER

The first and most obvious sign of trouble is the water becoming cloudy, as normally it is never changed. The cloudiness may be one of three colours: white, brown, or green (sometimes turning to yellow).

White cloudiness in the aquarium water is dangerous; it often means that for some reason the oxygen content of the water is too low and the carbon dioxide content is too high. Perhaps there are too many (or too big) fish that are taking the oxygen out of the water quicker than the air is replacing it; it may be a dead fish, snail, mussel, or other decomposing matter that is fouling the tank; it may be something dissolving in the water, for example, a harmful rock, shell or ornament, or it may be the temperature of the water has risen, so automatically reducing the water oxygen content and causing overcrowding and white cloudiness. In any event, white cloudiness has to be tackled at once or the fish will die; it is therefore essential to find the cause, calling in the specialist if necessary, and to change one-third of the water at a time, replacing with fresh water of the *same temperature*. The water is

27

changed with an ordinary clean jug or it can be siphoned, whichever is easier.

One complication arises in that green water, dealt with below, appears white in its initial stages, but if the fish show signs of distress it is safe to assume that the clouding of the water is, in fact, white, and to take the foregoing precautions. Obvious distress signals are detailed under heading (15) page 32.

Brown cloudiness is nearly always caused by dirt or by excess food that has not been eaten and lies around the tank, often turning the sand black. Sand not properly washed, too much sediment at the bottom which should be siphoned off, decaying leaves of plants, or some such cause. Lack of sufficient growing plants is also a contributory cause. Brown cloudiness is unsightly but not particularly dangerous in the first instance, although prolongation of this condition can encourage disease.

Green cloudiness is healthy. Under the action of excess light (sunlight, daylight or artificial) microscopic life is born which is green in colour; suspended in the water this causes it to turn green, or it can settle to become green slime over the sand, rocks, plants, glass, etc., or even as green strips on the sides. The fish will thrive on the green algae, unless excessive, as is emphasized in the chapter on breeding, but not on 'blanket-weed' described in the section on ponds.

Nevertheless, green is not pleasant to view and should not be permitted in a show tank; the cure is simple. Cut down the amount of light received by the aquarium, whether that light be sunlight, daylight or artificial. Of course, if the light is reduced too much the plants will not grow. The green algae already formed can be cleared in two to four days by adding special chemicals or one grain by weight of potassium permanganate to every 36 litres of water (any chemist will weigh out the correct amount). There should be no need to do more than change one third of the water afterwards, by siphoning off from the bottom. If no fish are present, a swarm of Daphnia will soon clean up the tank by the simple method of eating all the algae. Strongly growing plants, and general cleanliness, make it more difficult for algae to appear in the tank.

Should the water turn yellow, however, the process has been

carried too far, and the water must be changed; the sudden death of the microscopic green algae, due, say, to heat, causes them to decompose and turn the water yellow, which means that the water is now foul and must be changed most urgently as even half an hour can be fatal.

UNSUSPECTED DANGERS

Sometimes it happens that an aquarium has been functioning perfectly for a long time and then suddenly goes wrong for no apparent reason. As would be the case with a motor car, the cause may be simple or complex and is best traced by a specialist, but some of the more usual factors are listed below:

1. Incorrect feeding, especially through lack of live foods or their substitutes. See appropriate chapter for details.
2. Bad condition of the tank:

    (*a*) Fish overcrowded? Too many (or too big) fish can be crammed into a tank for a while but sooner or later will fall sick.

    (*b*) Dirt in a tank aggravates overcrowding. Excess food is nearly always the cause of dirt that lies about the tank as brown sediment. In bad instances the sand becomes black.

    (*c*) If the aquarium temperature is consistently kept too high, or too low, the fish will be weakened, even to the point of sickness and of death.

    (*d*) Too strong or too prolonged a light shining on the tank can be as tiring for fish as for humans. They, too, need some shade or at least some periods of darkness (say, at night). Shelter can be provided by clumps of plants or by rocks arranged in the form of a bridge or of a T. Furthermore, fish that are feeling out of sorts will be able to retire into these places for rest and privacy.

    (*e*) The plants should be healthy and be sufficient in number properly to do their work.
3. The presence of paint (even in the house next door), varnish, strong bath salts, disinfectants, D.D.T., strong-smelling oil-containing matter, some kitchen smells, are

definitely harmful as the water absorbs these foreign elements to the distress of the fish. The importance of this point can be underlined by the following cases our staff at *Fish Tanks Ltd.*, have been called upon to solve.

(*a*) The aquarium was kept near a bathroom where strong Dettol was used for ten days; the fish fell ill.

(*b*) The chauffeur used to feed the fish and to rearrange the rocks; he came straight from the garage and his hands smelt of petrol and oil.

(*c*) The room had beautiful parquet flooring which was regularly polished; the accumulative effect of the polish smell was too much for the tank.

(*d*) The over-careful aquarist who washed his hands thoroughly before touching his tank; unfortunately he used strongly scented soap.

The above are mere examples, they show the attention that must be paid to this point. In nearly every case, however, a tell-tale scum (often oily) on the top of the aquarium water indicated the cause of the trouble; but this does not always apply, Dettol for example leaves virtually no scum.

The top of the water will have to be skimmed, and even part changed (with water of the same temperature) as detailed in Chapter 3, until about one-third of the water *from the top* has been removed – if possible without being stirred. A further protection is to cover the top of the aquarium with a sheet of glass or some such substitute until the danger has passed.

4. Too much mastic or putty on the inside of the tank and in contact with the water is inadvisable. Mastic on the outside does not matter.

5. Harmful substances introduced into the tank from outside. Apart from the non-aquatic rocks, ornaments, etc., these can be brought into the tank by dirty hands, newly-applied nail varnish, dirty cloths, dusters or tools that have been kept in a drawer with tins of paint, etc. It is surprising how strongly the hands can smell of the kitchen, the garage, or of a tin of varnish.

6. Disease introduced by new fish, plants, or live foods.

30

Unsuitable fish can engender disease if they take up too much oxygen, because they are too big, or are fish more used to the running water of streams (in the case of cold-water fish); some types of fish, too, do not live quietly in a community tank and are bullies or even killers. Fish accustomed to aeration will suffer in still water.

7. Something wrong with the water temperature, especially in the case of tropicals; too wide fluctuations, faulty wiring, or perhaps simply that the heater or thermostat has got buried by drifting sand. Perhaps, too, the heating elements are no longer in good condition or are actually giving off gases. Some thermometers are not quite as reliable as one would like and they, too, should be checked in case they are giving false readings.

8. Water enemies, as described in Chapter 13, should not be in the tank.

9. Fish urine is not visible but results in excess toxic ammonia compounds which affect the gill plates of the fish, causing red inflammation and ultra-quick breathing. The fish hangs at unusual angles, even quivers, and later has blotches on its body. Water must be changed, urgently, as there is no other way of removing the urine, and aeration can be increased.

10. An imbalance of plant life usually shows as (a), patches of black sand developing round the plant roots because harmful nitrites have been over produced rather than the helpful nitrates or, (b), white precipitate grains forming on the leaves during the night and disappearing gradually by day.

In both cases the balance of the tank is altogether too precarious because there are either too many fish for the few plants, or the reverse. Even one extra hour of sunlight or a few extra grains of dirt (e.g. food) could cause havoc in this situation. Change the water, get more plants (or fish) and adjust the duration/strength of the top lighting to encourage plant growth. A slight increase of 10 per cent growth may correct matters.

If the tank water is too acid, as shown by a pH reading (percentage of hydrogen) of below 7·0 on the indicators widely available in the shops, then a plant fertilizer should be used.

11. In addition to the pH factor of acid/alkaline just mentioned, is the DH factor of 'degree of hardness' of the water. Waters vary widely, e.g. at Manaus on the River Negro in South America, where so many Neons and Cardinal fish come from, the DH is 4–6; in London it is 12–18. A sudden transfer at the end of a jet aeroplane journey to a totally different DH throws such a strain on the delicately balanced membranes of the fish gill plates that they collapse and the fish usually dies in less than an hour – the actual time depending on the violence of the fluctuation.

12. Water stratification means that there are insufficient fish and/or aeration to give an even, all-over temperature so that fish are being forced to go through different strata of temperatures as they swim up or down. Particularly vulnerable are the base-dwellers like the Cat fish who normally stay in the bottom 3cm. of water. Make quite sure that your heater is completely flat in this bottom 3cm. which is therefore heated. Alternatively, adjust your aeration.

13. Is your filter clean? Is it big enough? Is the rate of flow fast enough, or are there too many eddies and unswept areas? A dirty filter merely pours back poisoned water, making matters worse.

14. Is there sufficient overhead shade/protection from the toplight? Are there enough nooks, crannies, clefts, ledges, covers, plant thickets, thick leaved plants? You need to cater for all types, including the weak, timid and infirm.

15. *Signs of fish distress*

(*a*) Drooping the fins, pale colour (fear/pain intensifies colours unnaturally), lack of appetite, lethargic.

(*b*) Head/tail hanging down, moping off into unusual parts of the tank (top swimmers coming down to mid-water, etc.), hiding in plants (often head first), making slow circles at the surface, tail down and mouth up seeking more oxygen (change water at once).

(*c*) Unusual darts to safety, pants, shivers, trying to bury

32

and hide or keeping its mouth open for too long. (Act at once to help. If you can't do better at least change the water.)

Or else:

(*d*) Boisterousness and bullying. Your fish may want a mate. It may be psychologically upset and want a home of its own, a cave, cleft, or a thick leaf, etc.

Persistent bullies can be temporarily isolated in a breeding trap or clean jam-jar half filled with tank water and floating on the tank water surface. It may just want better, more varied foods. Constipation shows as long, thread-like excreta hanging down from the vent – give (laxative) live daphnia foods.

16. *Try to understand your fish*

They do their very best to tell you their preferences, to make friends with you, and to help you to realize that their shapes and colours are positive clues to their ideal environment. As you are responsible for their well-being, please note the following points:

(*a*) Body long, slim and torpedo shaped. A fast/far swimmer needing lots of free waters.

(*b*) Torpedo body, but with prominent finnage. A quick accelerator which will dart out to forage rather than go in for far ranging swims. Less free waters, frequently interspersed with foliage, would be preferred.

(*c*) Eyes clear, prominent, perhaps rimmed with a strong colour (like red, for instance). The waters would need to be clean and clear for all-round vision. Brightly lit. Murky, cloudy tanks are no more welcome to them and no more conducive to good health than persistent smog is to us.

(*d*) Longitudinal, light sheeny markings on the body. Require both free waters, and strong currents (so step up aeration). The light sheen calls for clean and bright soft waters (nicely filtered, and of DH 6–8 rather than 12–18). Often the digestive tracks are short so that food is eliminated quickly – which means that the fish should be fed three times a day. The strong currents of the filters should eliminate all droppings quickly.

(*e*) High body colours. Like the Neon, the Cardinal, the Glow-light. Their native habitat of shallow streams are rich with fallen vegetation, over which flow pronounced currents creating DH 4–6 and pH 6·8 with very low parts per million of dissolved solids. Their high body colours are perfect camouflage in the piercing shafts of strong sunlight which break through the overhanging vegetation. So please reproduce overhanging protection, and alternating light and shade.

(*f*) Smudged, but high-coloured body markings. Like the Rosy Barb, the Nigro Barb, the Tiger Barb. Similar to the above Neons these fish need overhead vegetation, but not quite so thickly hung, to give areas of light and shade, rather than piercing shafts. Less timid than the Neons, the Barbs like to move into a brightly lit area and bask/browse for a while before returning to the shade. The less fastidious fish (indicated by untidy smudges and less clean cut markings) is more able to endure poor diets and survive better in murky waters.

(*g*) Rounded Body. The rounder the body, the deeper the waters required, examples are Scats and Angels. Also indicates a fish which sallys forth from protective clefts or reed thickets, rather than staying in the open for prolonged periods. If either of the fish mentioned becomes aggressive, then you have upset it psychologically by not providing a home of its own, or by depriving it of congenial mates. Its built in shyness then turns to aggressive defensiveness. But there are differences. The Scats have smudged untidy markings indicating wide tolerance to varied waters, and can go from full marine, through brackish, to fresh waters. The clean-cut, bright sheeny Angels with clear eyes, rimmed with red, denote a more evolved fish requiring better conditions.

(*h*) Barbels and Feelers. The differences continue with the barbels in the mouth of the Scats which denote a lack of discrimination in food and are even a mark of greed. Scats are constantly foraging, and eat anything/anywhere. The long, delicate, finely draped feelers of the Angels demand higher standards; their small mouths pick daintily at chosen mouthfuls. They are apt to go on hunger strike if not provided with satisfactory food. If the feelers begin to splinter, to go ragged, then the tank conditions are becoming intolerable and you should improve them.

The Barbs mentioned above, also have barbels, and also forage to the point of greed. They therefore eliminate a lot, and often, and soon foul sluggish waters; your filters will need to reproduce the full-flow of the native streams these fish are used to.

(*i*) Mouth. If forward pointing, i.e. terminal, then the fish tends to be a mid-water dweller. Upward pointing (super terminal) and downward pointing (sub terminal) denote the top and bottom waters preferred respectively. Hatchets, for example, with their strong pectoral (breast) fins, super terminal mouths, and flat backs not only swim on top, they will readily leap along (or even above) the surface to catch their food. Hence their tanks need to be covered about 8cm. above the water surface to prevent them from falling/jumping out. Barbels in the mouth of the Barbs stress their constant search for food. Aggressive mouths denote danger to others. Strong suckers on the mouth indicate an ability to hang or suck along as they feed off ledges, rocks, plants or glass and to withstand strong currents as they cling. Fast flowing aeration is helpful. Most sucker mouths are used to feed off green algae, which is produced by strong light, so that requirement must be provided. Such vegetarians dislike meat.

(*j*) Backs and tummy. The more arching the back and the flatter the tummy the more the fish will stay down at the sandy bed – look at the extreme example of the catfish. Note that the clearer, more finely marked Leopard catfish requires clean waters and less base mulm/debris than the darkly smudged varieties. The more arched the back is, the slower a swimmer the fish will be. Some are seldom capable of more than a darting acceleration for a short burst.

(*k*) Eyes. The wider apart they are, the less light they like and they are more likely to be crepuscular – dawn or dusk seeing them venture out – like the sucking catfish, e.g. the plectosomus. Hence they tend to stay deep down, and to hide up by day. In strong light, without a home to cling to, the fish would die; especially if a lack of fast-flowing filtration had made the tank dirty.

(*l*) Killie fish like the Aphysomenion – excessive high colours, excessive finnage. They live and die in excessive haste as birth, maturity, spawning and death all have to be crowded into a few short months when the rains fill the mud pools and before the sun dries them out.

General body appearance of defence or of attack
If the mouth is small and the body is laterally compressed with long feelers and camouflaged colours (rather than of garish colouring like the Dwarf Gourami) the fish is likely to prefer to shoal for defence, and would wilt if left alone, especially if unprotected by rock clefts or reed thickets.

If like the Black Widow the mouth is business-like, but the body has heavy trailing downwards then it is likely to be a mid water dweller which stays under protective large/broad/wide leaves to sally forth for food. It snaps back firmly in self-defence and does not depend so much on shoaling; but stops well short of being aggressive. If your particular specimen is over liable to snap, then what are you doing wrong? The fault will be yours, not that of the fish.

Every word of the above points is important. For instance, one very competent aquarist who had 'greenfingers', and could keep fish without trouble, suddenly found things going all wrong; the fish were not overcrowded, were well-fed, in a long established and correctly balanced tank, beautifully clean, the plants were thriving, nothing new had been intro-duced for two months, and yet something was wrong. No, there had been no paint, disinfectant or varnish used – the aquarist was quite, quite, sure. In the end, the cause of the trouble was found: aquarium tools were being kept in a drawer with long-forgotten, half-empty tins of paint.

When there is trouble, there *is* a cause, no matter how obscure, and it can be found and remedied.

CONCLUSION

In general, the aquarium which has been expertly balanced in the first place should seldom go wrong.

The causes of trouble detailed here are out-of-the-ordinary ones. It is quite untrue to maintain that a cocktail bar, a public house, a busy hotel foyer, or any other crowded place is unsuitable for an aquarium. *Fish Tanks Ltd.* have not only installed them in such places but have kept them in such rigorous conditions as the toy department of famous stores – even at Christmas time – and at exhibitions, where literally thousands of people crowd past every hour of the day for weeks on end, and when the heat and the dust have been so bad that the staff in charge of the exhibitions had to be changed every few hours to avoid headaches and sore throats. And yet the fish did not suffer. So, given a fair chance and proper knowledge, fish will prove themselves trouble-free, hardy and a source of great pleasure.

6

Breeding and Rearing
Tropical Fish

Some fish give birth direct to fully-formed live baby fish; these are called viviparous. From them many interesting cross-breeds, or hybrids, have been evolved. Others lay eggs first in the normal way; these can be adhesive or not, can be scattered, or carefully guarded. The nests are of all kinds, including floating air bubbles with the eggs individually wrapped in these hygienic containers.

The difficulty in breeding is so often not in the mating and spawning, but in the successful rearing of the fry, and this is one of the main reasons it is so much easier to breed the viviparous kinds as the eggs are fertilized and hatched inside the mother's body and are thus virtually past the danger stage when born. Breeding problems vary from the extremely simple, say in the case of a live-bearing Guppy, to the practically impossible in the case of the more rare egg-layers like the Kuhlii Eel. For this reason detailed information is given under the descriptions of the individual fish at the end of the book, and the remarks here will deal with the general methods, applicable more or less to all occasions.

There is no particular season for the breeding of tropicals because it is nearly always possible to provide ideal conditions; the supply of live foods, and of sunlight, are two reasons why summer-time is favoured, but winter breeding is quite practicable.

BREEDING TANK

The breeding tank itself is often quite shallow, perhaps 15cm.–23cm. deep, but it should not be too small, say, not less than 36cm. long by 20cm. high by 25cm. wide, as many fish, such as the live-bearing Molly, get nervous and excited when confined in small spaces and these nervous disorders can cause a disturbing number of complications. A large breeding tank is not necessary, although it is essential for the successful rearing of the young. This was one of the points mentioned in Chapter 1 as being vital for the future health of the babies; overcrowding is bad in that all the fish are retarded in growth and strength; in fact Nature often takes a hand, causing a fatal epidemic and so destroying the weaker fish, leaving the others sufficient room for proper growth. For rearing, too, as distinct from breeding, the deepest tank – say 30cm. – is advantageous since it encourages the development of better specimens.

When plants are being used the planted side of the breeding tank should always be towards the light, because that is the way the fry will instinctively turn in order to seek hiding-places and protection.

BREEDING TRAP

In many instances a breeding trap is used inside the rearing tank, so as to separate the parents or parent from the eggs or live young. These traps are of many types – V-shaped, a layer of glass rods spaced apart, perforated celluloid sheet, finely meshed wire – or any method allowing the eggs or live babies to drop through small gaps into the rearing tank, gaps that are just big enough for that, but too small to allow the adult fish to follow. As is well known, the parents so often eat the young fish or their eggs; where this does not apply, the breeding trap is quite unnecessary.

CHOOSING AND CONDITIONING
THE PARENTS

The parents should be chosen with great care, the individual fish being the best obtainable, having regard to size, shape, colour, finnage, and so on; further, the prospective parents should like each other, that is, harmonize. The best way to ensure this is to place a group of adult fish in a tank and wait for them to 'pair off', the chosen ones being transferred to separate tanks.

With the egg-layers, two or even more males are often used with one female. If the sexes are kept separately, brought to breeding condition as described below, and are then placed in the mating tank at night, they will often spawn next morning. Better still, if they can be put together at dawn in the morning they will tend to spawn almost at once. It is usual to put the weaker fish (often the female) in first, so that it is already feeling at home before meeting the other fish.

Green water and/or two hours daily of sunlight are helpful in bringing the parents to breeding condition. Live foods, too, are practically essential: Daphnia, Tubifex worms, chopped earthworms, brine shrimps' eggs, etc., can be given twice a day, enough at one feeding to last about 15–30 minutes. Too many white worms will tend to make the fish fat and reluctant to spawn. The rule is, therefore, to feed well but not too heavily.

As explained in the chapter on feeding the frequency really depends on the water temperature; below 21°C. for tropical fish their appetite is sluggish, at 24°C. it is very keen, after 28°C. the lowered oxygen content of the water reduces the appetite again. Similarly, for coldwater fish the temperatures vary approximately from 13°C. to 18°C. and 22°C. – approximately, because various types of fish have varying optimum temperature ranges.

The temperature of the mating tank is often raised one to three degrees C. when the adult fish are introduced, as this is bound to help spawning, and this higher temperature can be maintained till the eggs are hatched and even for the early stages of the fry. Restraint must be exercised, as explained in Chapter 1, lest the prolonged increase in temperature cause the fry to grow so fast as to be weakened. Once spawning is completed, the parents are separated from the eggs or young – except the chiclids, or, in the case of the labyrinth breathers, leave the male only with the nest for about a week. (Types of fish are described in a later part of the book.)

7

Infusoria

THE mating and spawning process is often easier than the rearing of the fry. The commonest difficulties are insufficient or unsuitable food at the early stages, and lack of space.

When the eggs are hatched, or the viviparous babies are born, in both instances a 'yolk sac' is attached to the fry with sufficient food for the initial period which may last from a few hours to two or three days, especially if supplemented by the addition to the tank of liberal quantities of green water, which is automatically rich in baby-food. The yolk-sac gone the hobbyist must assume responsibility, especially for the egg-layed fry, and this is done by providing infusoria both *early* and *constantly*. Infusoria are living organisms in water on which the fish can live until they have grown enough to eat normal foods.

Infusoria can be prepared in dozens of ways, some of which are now listed:

1. Outside leaves of a lettuce placed in water and left in bright light, preferably sunlight, for three or four days; when the water, especially round the leaves, becomes white or milky the culture is ready. One drop examined under a microscope will be seen to be teeming with life, appearing as continuously moving dustlike particles. Pond water (free of all enemies) is better than tap water. After about four days, the culture 'dies' – that is, bacteria predominate over the more useful organisms; hence the need for several overlapping cultures to be started three days apart. About three bruised leaves per quart of water should be used; bruising helps to hasten the decomposition of the leaves and the birth of infusoria.

2. Other vegetable matter can be used to make a culture; for example – finely sliced potatoes left in water till they begin to smell. Cow dung gives especially small infusoria that can be used for tiny fish like the Ambassis Iala (Glass Fish).

41

3. A quick method is to pour boiling water on chopped-up hay, leaving it to stand in the sunlight till the water becomes light brown.

4. Using some such mixture as the peel of one potato, one split pea, one yellow skin of a banana, one spinach leaf, thirty drops of milk, one tiny piece of fish (3cm. by 3cm. by 1cm.) to about 10 litres of water; leave in the light as described above.

All the above four cultures smell and go foul after three to five days. (For temperature regulation, see below.)

5. To overcome this difficulty the cultures can be sterilized, as follows:

§ Slow boil for twenty minutes a mixture of almost any vegetable matter, such as chopped hay, brown rice, oatmeal, split peas, milk (condensed or bottled), lettuce, potato, etc. This slow boil will kill the bacteria of putrefaction; the mixture should be left to cool for a day and should be carefully protected against dust. We may call this 'the culture'.

At the same time, similarly boil for twenty minutes separate quarts of water, each containing one of the above ingredients (hay, lettuce, potato, etc.), pour into separate jars and leave to cool also for a day, protected from the dust.

Next add six or seven drops of the culture to each jar, keep protected from dust, and leave in the bright light (sunlight preferred) for three days. The water will be teeming with life, and the infusoria is ready for use.

The great advantages of this method are:

(a) The different infusoria of oatmeal, hay, lettuce, etc., are separate, and fish will soon show which particular one they prefer.

(b) The preparations will not 'die' under two weeks.

(c) There is practically no smell.

(d) Risk of infection is greatly reduced, especially if all implements (including the hands!) are sterilized before going from one preparation to another. This risk of infection is very real.

All the five methods of making infusoria, listed above, are affected by temperature. If the infusoria water is at 27°C. or above, the cycle of events is accelerated, so that the culture is sooner ready for use, but it 'dies' more quickly, too, as the bacteria outstrip the useful living organisms. Similarly, under 16°C. the development is needlessly slow. Hence a temperature of 18–20°C. is best. Remember that infusoria, like fish, do not like a sudden change of temperature; if taken from a culture of 20°C. and put straight into an aquarium of 26°C. they will tend to suffer. Indeed infusoria might even die before the fry eat them during the course of the day.

The infusoria water will have to be replaced as used from the jars; in the case of the first four methods pond or tap water is best, and for the sterilized preparations boiled water that has cooled should be used.

If no infusoria is ready, the fry will almost certainly suffer, but the following substitutes will help:

Feed the fry with drops of a liquid made by adding very little water (or heavily diluted milk) to mashed Daphnia, brine shrimps, cyclops, the yellow of a hardboiled egg, chopped earthworms, powdered oatmeal, etc. The danger of clouding the water, or even of fouling it, is ever present and in this method the use of scavenging snails is advisable.

HOW TO FEED THE INFUSORIA TO FISH

Probably this is best done by the 'drip method'. A jar containing the infusoria water is fixed above the tank level and this water is allowed to drip into the tank through a rubber tube, the rate of flow being regulated by a pinch-cock – a type of clip that can be adjusted to squeeze the rubber tube at any given pressure; the bigger the opening left inside the tube the greater the flow of infusoria.

The question of how much infusoria to give is a tricky one. Obviously it must be enough, equally obviously too much may engender disease in the tank, and bacteria cannot easily be siphoned off like uneaten food. Differences in culture strength, in water temperature, in age, size and number of fry, all govern this vexed question of the quantity to feed. The only advice is to use common sense but infusoria must be given early and constantly until the fry have outgrown the need for it. The bellies of the fry should always be full. Infusoria should be

43

continued until the fry are about three times their original size. Stopping too soon kills fry – continuing too long stops their growth. Size, not time, is the important factor.

The really difficult stage in development has now been reached: The fry are too big for infusoria and as yet too small for ordinary foods.

'Micro' has been introduced from Sweden, thanks largely to the kindness of Mrs. Morten Grindal, of Solna; these minute worms are small enough to be fed to the fry at their present difficult stage. Alternatively, rotifers, newly-hatched brine shrimps, dry powdered food, will all do and, at a slightly later stage, finely sifted Daphnia.

Watch with a magnifying glass – if the fry spit out the food, it is still too big for them.

They should, however, be fed very frequently at this stage, say up to eight times a day, and a limited amount of sediment should be allowed to accumulate as it helps to grow the plants and infusoria; of course, the danger of siphoning off fry as well as sediment is very real and will call for both patience and skill.

To repeat: all the remarks in this chapter are applicable only in the general sense; Neon Tetras, for example, like a spotlessly clean tank for their fry; and reference should be made to the end of the book for detailed points of advice. However, this chapter will serve as a general guide for the enthusiast who has persevered thus far.

PROFESSIONALLY PREPARED SUBSTITUTES OF THE ABOVE INFUSORIA

Several of these are now on the market, ready for instant use. The most widely sold is like a tube of toothpaste from which a little is squeezed. Also obtainable are tubes of dried infusoria that rapidly mature in water.

8

Types of Eggs and their Care

As has already been emphasized, different types of fish have varying preferences and methods of laying their eggs, but the following general remarks will serve as some guide.

1. ADHESIVE EGGS
Fish will often spend care and trouble to choose the spot where these adhesive eggs will be laid. Broad leaves of a strongly-growing plant like Sagittaria or Cryptocoryne are used, but especially the underside of the Sagittaria; so too are the insides of small flower pots, or even the hollow of a conveniently shaped rock; some fish, of course, merely scatter their adhesive eggs which should be caught by bushy plants grouped in bunches.

2. NON-ADHESIVE EGGS
These are either scattered, as for example on thickets of plants, noticeably those with fine leaves like myriophyllum, ambulia, cabomba, or even hair grass, which serve partly to catch the eggs but more especially to hide them, and the newly-hatched fry, from the dangers of being eaten. Alternatively, the eggs are placed in carefully formed and guarded nests; especially is this so with the chiclids, which often use a hollow in the sand which they will guard against all comers. The same is true of the very interesting bubble-nest builders, as detailed in the appropriate chapter.

HOW TO MOVE THE EGGS
In lifting out the plants holding the eggs it is most unwise to subject them to sudden temperature changes or to expose them to the air. A simple plan is to place a bowl under these plants, raise the bowl, taking care to keep the plants, roots if any, and eggs submerged, and so to move them still in their same water to the rearing tank of the same temperature.

General questions such as whether the water should be 'old', green, or what its pH or DH should be, or whether the floor should be spotlessly clean or covered with some mulm, can only be answered in the case of particular breeding adult fish. They are mentioned here simply so that they can be noted by the hobbyist, helping him to overcome unexplained difficulties. The fry will need 'mature' water for their growth.

The same applies also to temperature and aeration, but it should be remembered, however, that fish accustomed to constant aeration will have to be taught gradually to do without it. Provided a tank is large enough, there should be no need for more than gentle aeration.

In all breeding routine, the question of cleanliness and the danger of infection will have to be watched most carefully. All nets, planting sticks, even the aquarist's hands, should be sterilized regularly. Ozonisers are increasingly used as the O_3 they emit kills bacteria; please don't make the dose too strong.

INFERTILE EGGS

Eggs that prove infertile, often becoming covered with fungus, should be removed if possible and an effort made to find out why they did not hatch in the normal way.

It is often found that some, or even many, eggs are covered with fungus but it is rare for all to be bad.

Snails eat eggs, and should always be removed from the breeding tank but not necessarily from the rearing tank where they will help to keep the bottom clean – they will not eat the fry.

Should the eggs be infertile the causes may be:
1. Temperature wrong.
2. Too much or too little light. Neons need 5 days of darkness.
3. Dirt.
4. Infected infusoria culture that breeds fish enemies or harmful bacteria as well as the normal ones. Clean and sterilize and, therefore, use another culture.
5. Unsuitable water that might contain harmful gases or matter. Filter the tap water through glass wool or fine sand, and through activated charcoal, such as Hydraffin (bought from specialist dealers); or use rainwater instead. Perhaps the water was too deep.
6. Check water pH and DH. If new water has been used, try

'seasoned' water, obtained by drawing from the tap and leaving in bright light (sunlight if possible) for a day; without disturbing the precipitate that will have formed at the botton, siphon off the water into another clean container and leave it there (again in the sunlight if possible) to mature for a further twenty-four to forty-eight hours. The siphoning gets rid of any insoluble or floating matter.

7. Eggs not fertilized: perhaps the pair of adults did not harmonize – suggest the use of additional males, say two or three males to one female.

8. Tank too small.

9. Scum on top of the water, or cold draughts as you lift the tank cover, can wreak havoc.

10. Aureomycin sufficient just to tinge the water (or methylene blue), coupled with light aeration should help.

FURTHER HINTS ON BREEDING

If the water in the shallow breeding tank is too low to hold an immersion thermostat comfortably, the latter can be immersed into a jar standing in the tank. Thus the water temperature of the tank will govern that of the water in the jar, so ensuring correct response by the thermostat.

In removing fry, it is advisable to use a fry-catcher, as netting may harm them. This is used in a scooping action, the fry being allowed to swim into the bowl.

Keep the water level of the rearing tank well below that of the tank sides as a protection against draughts. A glass cover is an additional protection against temperature fluctuations and dust – important at this fry stage.

CONCLUSION

Breeding is not so much a matter of hard and fast rules as of 'feeling' and common sense; conditions, waters, fish, foods, sunlight and the like all vary from place to place and from time to time. Patience is essential, as periodical failures and disappointments are quite certain to occur.

Breeding Traps

All manner of other aids will make life easier for you, and save buying a second tank.

9
Breeding of Aquarium Coldwater Fish

A CONTROVERSIAL point should be mentioned at the start: Should the breeding be done in a pond or in an aquarium?

The two really great advantages of the pond are its relatively large volume of water, and in good weather its abundance of natural foods for the young fish.

The disadvantages lie in the whims of the British climate; apart from extremes of heat or frost and ice, the normal temperature variations are very great indeed, 10°C. being quite frequent, and there is little the average aquarist can do to control them. Furthermore, these changes are rapid, occurring within a few hours. So, too, is there a great discrepancy in the amount of light, especially sunlight, and an evenly spread supply is almost hopeless.

But these disadvantages have their attenuating factors. Although the atmospheric temperature changes very quickly, a fairly large volume of water is affected only slowly and cushions the fish from the worst of the shock. This is particularly so if the water is about a metre deep. Secondly, the fish seem to have a natural ability to pick out the coming fine weather and will normally spawn just at the start of a good spell; they cannot, of course, *make* good weather and the fine spells in Britain have a nasty tendency to fade off after a very few days.

Just as natural foods are abundant in open ponds, so too on occasions are fish lice and water enemies; the pond should, therefore, be capable of being thoroughly cleaned.

Naturally enough, no other fish, apart from the selected parents, must be present to spoil the quality of the spawnings. This also means that the pond should be periodically emptied to ensure that overlooked eggs or fry from previous matings have not remained behind to grow and to interbreed with the chosen parents.

If the aquarist has decided to do the breeding in ponds, he may still be well advised to hatch the eggs in an aquarium and to keep the fry indoors for the first crucial ten weeks. A pond that is more or less bare, except for ideal spawning plants at the shallow edge, practically forces the fish to spawn on these plants which can then easily be removed to an aquarium; fresh supplies of plants should be available to keep up with the spawnings.

It is important that these bunches of plants be frequently rinsed to shake off dead algae or any other such foreign matter that could later prevent the eggs adhering properly.

If the parents are not separated from the eggs many of these will be eaten. Even more important, once the fry have appeared it is the slower swimming ones that get less of the food and are more subject to being attacked; the slower swimmers are usually those with the longer finnage – the very fish that the aquarist would most like to save.

Obviously, spawning starts with good-quality parents that have been separately brought up to the best possible condition. It is a bad mistake to use inferior fish as the resulting fry are just not worth the trouble. Each prospective parent should be known to have come from good stock and, even if not perfect in itself, be known to be capable of producing good young.

Sexing the fish is difficult. In exotic specimens, such as the Veiltail and the Fantail, the males are often as full bodied as the females. Only at breeding condition do the male tubercles appear as raised white dots on the gill plates, and on the pectoral fins; an absence of these dots might mean that the fish is a female or that it is a male not ready to breed. Once spawning starts, however, the females can easily be picked out as they are vigorously chased and nuzzled by the males.

The breeding season normally begins at the end of April. Two or more males should be used to 'drive' each female in the well-known chase which may last a few hours or even two or three days. Thus frequent replacements of plants to catch the eggs as they are scattered and plenty of swimming room are essential. In the aquarium a good supply of aeration helps. The water temperature should not be below 16°C. or above 27°C.; in the one fish tend to be sluggish, in the other they

49

lack oxygen. 20–22°C. is ideal for the driving, and bright light, especially sunlight, is appreciated.

The eggs, transparent, adhesive and the size of a pin-head, are laid in clusters, no two individual eggs being in contact. Within twenty-four to forty-eight hours the infertile ones turn opaque, almost milky; there always seem so many of these that the aquarist despairs of any hatching out, but patience and diligence are usually rewarded.

21–24°C. is a good temperature for the incubation, and in four days fry should appear. They are free swimming within forty-eight hours and will need green water, infusoria, etc., as described in detail in the chapters on feeding. Most of all they will need plenty of space. Warmth, space and ample foods are all essential. As many as one thousand fry can result from a good spawning, so that the problem of space is pressing; it is most strongly advised to pick out the best specimens as soon as is practicable and to concentrate on them alone, disposing of the others. Aeration is helpful right from the commencement of the incubation period.

A temperature that is excessively high forces the growth of the fish and seriously weakens their constitution. It sometimes overdevelops the finnage too.

All along the line inferior fish should be removed. For example, with fantails, veiltails and Moors the ones with only single tails instead of the prized forked tails can be detected well before they are fourteen days old and should be taken out. Later, as body shapes develop, the poor quality should be ruthlessly sacrificed. By the time three months have passed the selection should have been completed.

Within two weeks the fry are past the infusoria stage and will swallow finely powdered dry foods, dried eggs, oatmeal, etc. Great care must be taken not to foul the water, which can often be part changed, especially if snails are not able to cope with the work. Another few days, and micro worms, finely sifted Daphnia (newly hatched brine shrimps fattened in green water) and not quite such powdered dry foods should be introduced. Within three to four weeks the last stage of tubifex and chopped white worms is reached. The worst danger is now over.

Meanwhile, the difficulty has been to get the fish to colour. The scales should be transparent so that a good body colour can be seen through them; often the scales remain opaque and a dark, uninteresting fish results.

If the parents have come from good stock, if the temperatures suggested above have been maintained, if ample space has been provided, if plenty of live foods were constantly given and if the Clerk of the Weather has kindly provided sunlight, then the fry should colour within eight months, some even within four months. A constant drip flow of water into the aquarium helps enormously. If a year goes by without the colour showing through then hope of obtaining a good fish cannot be high.

It is sometimes suggested that the aquarium bottom painted a bright colour such as yellow or red influences the colour development of the fry, and there is some evidence of this. General conditions, including the surrounding colours and their inter-action with sunlight, do influence the fry development and this suggestion should not be dismissed too lightly.

Fry born in May/June and reaching eight cm. by the late autumn can usually winter out of doors for the hardier types such as shubunkins and fantails. August/September hatchings should be reared indoors. Veiltails, moors, and lionheads are far better kept in aquaria. Once the fry have successfully survived one winter they are ready to take an active part themselves in this question of breeding; the best age, however, is some two years later when they have grown considerably.

The above descriptions apply to coldwater aquarium fish in general. It is remembered that strictly *pond* fish such as goldfish, carp, rudd, orfe, tench, etc., are not being discussed, although their breeding conforms in the main with that detailed above.

At the end of the book are illustrated some of the best aquarium coldwater fish, together with some additional comments on them.

10

Plants

PLANTS are often classified as tropical and coldwater, but it is proposed here to divide them into aquarium or pond plants because hot-house-grown (or tropical) plants will root in a coldwater tank kept in the normal living-room of a home, especially if an aquarium toplight is functioning. Strictly coldwater plants, on the other hand, are normally considered to be those that will thrive out in the open, winter or summer.

There is an important amount of interchange between the two categories, but the main distinction remains: those grown with the aid of artificial heat, e.g. in a hothouse, are for an aquarium, and those grown in the open are for a pond. It should be noted that although the same plant is often found both indoors and out, the pond one tends to be larger and coarser and not exactly the same as the one in the aquarium.

THE NEED FOR PLANTS

Plants are not merely decorative and pleasing in appearance but are essential to complete the scientific balance of the modern aquarium. This has been dealt with in Chapter 2 and need not be enlarged upon.

Further, the majority of community fish have a definite preference for a planted tank where they can find shade, privacy, and hiding-places when they are feeling out of sorts or are anxious to evade the attentions of a particular fish, be it a bully, a rival, or too ardent a suitor. In spawning and in the rearing of young, of course, plants play a very definite and important part.

CARE OF AQUARIUM PLANTS

As previously mentioned, plants in a community tank need light. They should be rooted in aquarium sand, but not too deeply, and loam, earth, etc., are not necessary for their

Anacharis

Sagittaria

Vallisneria

growth. Loam can breed harmful bacteria unless sterilized, and if this is done then the loam is of little use to the plants; after all, part of the plants' function in a balanced tank is to 'absorb' the droppings of the fish – these fertilizing media being broken up by the plants – simultaneously promoting their own growth and materially helping to dispose of the droppings.

Propagation is done in two ways. *Vallisneria* and similar plants send out runners which develop into new roots that can be broken off and grown separately; *Myriophyllum* and *Ludwigia* and such others have cuttings taken from them at the nodes, and these will root of their own accord when planted.

Lead weights wrapped round the base are sometimes used to prevent the newly transferred plants from floating to the surface of the water, but they are very liable to damage the plants unless used most carefully; in any case, a little patience and a sand depth of 3cm. should make weights quite unnecessary. If planting pots or trays are favoured, they should be big enough and deep enough.

A final reminder about these lovely aquatic greens is to keep them wet; if they are allowed to dry even momentarily, for example when being transferred or while in the process of being planted, they will suffer for weeks, in fact they will sometimes shrivel and die. Also great care must be taken if, for any reason, the aquarium is being disinfected. The plants can easily be damaged by being rinsed in water that is too hot or in a disinfectant that is too strong. One quarter grain by weight of potassium permanganate in $4\frac{1}{2}$ litres of water makes a strong enough solution to wash off most parasites from the leaves.

Planting effects are more decorative if done in thickets and not in single stems. Obviously, the thickets should not be congested so that the individual stems do not have enough room to grow, four to eight in a bunch is reasonable. Provided that the fish can swim about freely there is little danger of the aquarium being overcrowded. The disadvantage of plants taking in oxygen at night, instead of giving it out, is not serious if the aquarium has a large enough air surface, as emphasized in Chapter 2.

It helps if the aquarium light is kept on for longer periods when the greenery is first planted so as to give the plants

Ambulia

Ludwigia

Cryptocoryne Willisii

Aponogeton Undulatum

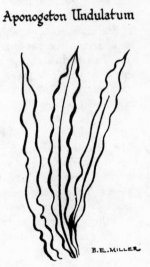

B.E.MILLER

a better chance to take root; this is particularly true in winter when natural growth is slow.

It is not proposed to describe the individual specimens in great detail, nor their various subdivisions, but the following general description of the more common plants may be of interest.

STRONG OXYGENATORS

These are plants that give off more oxygen than most. *Vallisneria* and *Sagittaria* are two of the best; from the illustrations it will be seen that they are very similar, *Sagittaria* being larger and coarser. *Vallisneria* leaves have a stripe down the centre dividing them into three nearly equal stripes of two shades of green. Both plants are normally found in three types, straight, twisted, and giant; there is also a *Dwarf Sagittaria*. Propagation is by runners that develop into roots.

Anacharis, propagated from cuttings and found in several varieties, especially *Elodea*, is another strong oxygenator.

OTHERS

All classified hereunder are propagated from cuttings, and are great favourites.

Ludwigia, some species of which have leaves that are tinged with red in the summer and autumn; *Hygrophila* is similar to the former but comparatively rare and of a very light and pleasant shade of green.

There are also bushy plants, such as *Myriophyllum*, *Ambulia* and *Cabomba*.

SPECIALS

Under this heading comes the tiny, delicate, lovely and hard-to-obtain *Hair Grass*.

Also there are plants that form a clump on their own, such as the broad-leaved, light green *Amazon Sword*, the serrated-edged *Aponogeton Undulatum*; and the very useful plants that will thrive in great heat and even in dim light – the *Cryptocorynes* particularly the *Cryptocoryne Willisi* and the *Cryptocoryne Becketti*.

FLOATING PLANTS

Numerous aquarium plants just float on the surface of the

1 Amazon Sword Plant

2 Hygrophila

3 Myriophyllum

water and are not rooted in any other medium, drawing their nourishment from the air and the water. The chief favourites among these plants are *Riccia*, *Azolla* and *Duckweed*. They are especially useful in providing shade in breeding, and as oxygenators, because they trap air bubbles from which the oxygen is absorbed into the water, especially at night.

CONCLUSION

This list makes no attempt to be complete or to go into the various species of each plant, nor does it differentiate between those having roots and those grown from bulbs; neither does it include quite well-known ones that are difficult to obtain, e.g. *Nuphar Lilies*, *Madagascar Lace Leaf*, *Acorus*, *Nitella*, *Indian Fern* and many others. Pond plants are described in the chapter on ponds.

WHY DO PLANTS DIE?

1. Their roots are too hot if the tank is above a radiator; a piece of protective asbestos over the radiator should normally suffice.
2. Too little, or unevenly spaced toplighting, especially if the tank is more than 50cm. deep.
3. Water too acid. See pH details on page 31.
4. Not enough fish to fertilize them.
5. Plants were allowed to get too dry after planting.
6. Not enough room to grow; e.g. thickets too thick, or lead weights too tight.
7. Wrong kind of plants, or more rarely, unsuitable water in the tank for that particular type of plant.
8. White flecks on the plants, especially in the morning, means too few fish and plants in the tank.
9. Black patches round the plant roots means too many harmful nitrates; tank needs a good clean up, and better balance.

Plant Fertilizers

Available in liquid and tablet form. All manner of vitalizers, for example, to help the newly transplanted cuttings or roots, are on sale; especially useful in winter when growth is normally slow.

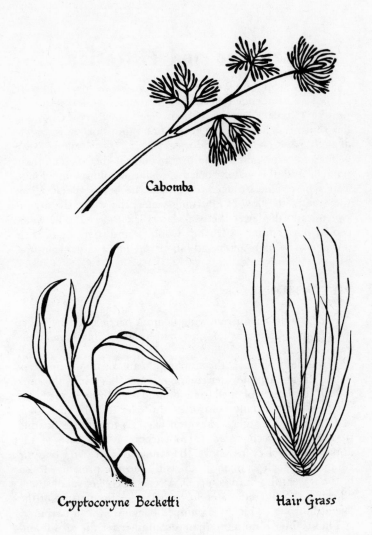

Cabomba

Cryptocoryne Becketti

Hair Grass

11

Aeration and Filtration

THE old air pumps were noisy and unsatisfactory, and were not recommended in earlier writings, as it certainly is possible to balance a tank without them. However the position has radically changed and really fine pumps are now widely available and are in general use.

The vibrator pumps, the piston pumps, the magnetic coil pumps, and the water cooled circulating pumps are found everywhere. The stronger the pump, the better the aeration, the greater the flow of returning water, the wider the area it sweeps, and the fewer the backwaters left to fester. The water cooled power filters will work wonders and soon repay their initial cost in happy fish and labour saving of tank clean-ups.

FILTRATION

A filter is a device for removing floating particles of the larger kind from aquarium water and even for absorbing some of the gases therein.

It is usual to connect the air pump to an 'air lift' by means of which the aquarium water can be pumped back into the tank after it has been siphoned from it and passed through the filter.

The filter normally consists of three layers: the first, such as fine sand, spun glass or cotton wool, is to remove floating particles; the second, activated carbon, is the core of the apparatus which even removes the gases and some of the organic compounds such as toxic products due to the presence of fish in the water; the third is merely a coarse layer of small stones allowing the filtered water to percolate to the bottom of the 'air lift' through which it is pumped back into the aquarium.

Thus a filter is no more than a container for the air lift and these three layers. It can be hung inside or outside the aquarium, depending on its size; the amount of work it can do is governed by its own area and by the rate of the water filtering through it.

The first layer of the filter shows the dirt and indicates the need for change, bearing as it does the brunt of the work by removing the larger floating particles. The sides of the filter, if it is being hung outside the tank, should be shielded from excess light, as should all connecting tubes, so as to discourage the formation of clogging algae.

The three layers must, of course, be packed down just tightly enough so that the water has to percolate through and not run down quickly; obviously, too, the layers will have to be of a reasonable area and of a sufficient thickness.

WHAT WILL THE FILTER DO?

The filter will remove floating particles and some gases, notably carbon-dioxide; it will also provide a form of aeration by circulating the water.

It will *not* remove algae, nor the sediment at the bottom of the tank, unless these have been stirred up and are suspended in the water; thus, water suffering from white or green cloudiness is not normally cleaned. Neither will the filter remove parasites that carry fish disease. Nor fish urine, which needs a urine skimmer.

Therefore, is it worth the trouble and expense? Frankly, yes. Like aeration, it is a useful adjunct.

SUB-GRAVEL FILTERS

Hidden below the sand level these catch the dirt and concentrate it in one place; the top sand appears clean, so does the water, *but* the dirt is still there in the tank until and unless you remove the whole filter and siphon off the dirt.

CORNER FILTERS

The filter is small, neat and cheap; it is so small that it soon becomes saturated and after that you are just fooling yourself! So please clean it often, or get a bigger one.

12

Cleaning the Tank and General Information

Keeping the tank clean is very important and quite simple, provided specialist advice is followed. Annoyingly enough, this advice consists mainly of a series of 'don'ts', all elaborated elsewhere but grouped below for the sake of convenience. Numbers two and three are especially important.

1. Don't buy your fish from a dealer whom you distrust or whose technical knowledge *as an aquarist* you feel is insufficient. (See pages 7 to 10.)
2. Don't buy too many fish or too few plants so that the balance of your tank is upset. (Pages 13 and 52.)
3. Don't, please don't, overfeed (page 23), but live food or its substitute is very helpful.
4. Place the aquarium in a sensible position; not backing on to a window (page 17), not in too bright a spot (page 28), not in a strong draught unless your dealer has been warned of that and has provided strong heaters.
5. Siphon off the bottom occasionally (page 20) and wipe the inside of the glass very, very gently.
6. See that the heating elements of the tropical tank work well.
7. Please re-read No. 16 on understanding your fish. (Page 33).

GENERAL INFORMATION

In the limited scope of this book there are several subjects that cannot be dealt with fully, and yet they ought at least to be mentioned. Accordingly they are given below, in the form of notes.

CLASSIFICATION OF FISH

The hundreds of fish suitable for an aquarium are divided into orders, the orders into families, the families into genera, and the genera into species. The most important order is Ostario-physi which contains the families of Characins (Black Widows, Beacons, Flames, Neons), of Carps (all the live bearers, Harlequins, Barbs, White Cloud Mountain Minnows), of Loaches (Kuhlii Eels) and of Catfish (Glass Catfish, Sucking Catfish, etc.).

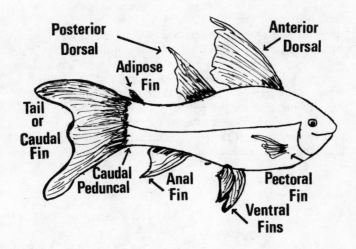

THE FINS ON A FISH

Most fish have seven fins of which four are paired, namely the pectoral or breast, and the ventral or pelvic; the eighth fin is called the adipose and is found mostly in Characins and in Catfish.

COMMUNITY FISH

All those described in this book are community fish; that means that they will live peacefully together. There are at least 400 types of these. The non-community fish are not dealt with here.

All labyrinth breeders need free air above water level which they can gulp, or they drown – please note this when carrying them home.

THE KINDS OF WATER

In different localities, water varies very considerably. Quite apart from the question of being hard or soft, the actual composition of the water varies with the amounts of salts, minerals and other such substances dissolved in it. These are usually referred to as 'TDS', or total dissolved solids. Water with a high TDS content is known as heavy and is not always good for fish, the opposite is known as 'light'. Unless the reader is preparing seriously to breed the more difficult kinds of fish he need not concern himself with this question at all.

pH denotes the degree of acidity or of alkalinity of the water and is measured on the following scale; the abbreviation pH denoting the percentage of 'Hydrogen ion concentration'.

	acid					alkaline			
←					neutral				→
6·0	6·2	6·4	6·6	6·8	7·0	7·2	7·4	7·6	7·8	8·0

Sodium bicarbonate added to the water will make it alkaline; acid sodium phosphate or very heavily diluted hydrochloric acid have the opposite effect.

Special sets are sold for measuring the changes in pH.

The ordinary aquarist need concern himself little about this subject unless he is proposing to breed very seriously with rare fish.

Water that has remained quite untouched is likely to give different pH readings at different times of the day because inter-action of the chemicals contained in it is always taking place. Further, an amount of water of pH 6·5 mixed with an equal quantity of pH 7·5 does not necessarily give a reading of pH 7·0 because one water may be 'buffered'. 'Buffered' water has a high mineral content and the influence of all these dissolved solids has to be overcome before there is an alteration in the pH reading. Tap water and rainwater are not usually 'buffered'.

DH or degree of hardness should also be noted, and it can easily be determined by one of the speciality kits widely sold. Basically the wild fish come from soft waters DH 2–8; home-bred town fish can be as high as DH 18. The adaptability of fish to this factor is enormous provided the fluctuation is done gradually, i.e. at least over some hours, if not days. 'When in doubt, soften the water' is a useful adage.

'Parts per million' of known salts/chemical contents is a further refinement, but requires fairly elaborate equipment to determine/maintain and is beyond the scope of this book.

Fluoride in drinking water is unfortunately becoming increasingly common as governments force this on to us with glib talk of saving teeth. It is a nerve gas, long used to tame wild animals, also used in war to make prisoners 'amenable', and its effect is deadly on fish. Boiling the water does not, repeat not, remove it, nor does ordinary filtration. A dreadful problem; no wonder people buy 'pure mountain waters' to drink!

MEASURING THE CAPACITY OF A TANK

The gallon capacity of an aquarium can be found by multiplying in feet the length × breadth × height × $6\frac{1}{4}$. For example an aquarium 2 ft. × 1 ft. × 1 ft. holds $12\frac{1}{2}$ gallons. This can be roughly converted into litres by multiplying by $4\frac{1}{2}$.

One gallon of water has 90,000 drops, weighs 10 lbs. and exerts pressure on the inside of the aquarium glass of 10 lbs. per square inch. (All these figures are approximate.) Metrically this would be approximately equal to $4\frac{1}{2}$ kilogrammes per 6·4 square centimetres.

SEALING A TANK

The sealing compound of mastic is often specially made to remain soft for two months. If the glass of the empty aquarium gets shaken away from the metal frame, during a journey for example, the internal water pressure of 10 lbs. per square inch will tend to push the soft mastic into any gaps that may have been caused and so to re-seal a leak. Once the water has been put in, a leak that is no greater than a drip will stop of its own accord as the mastic is pushed into position gradually over twelve to forty-eight hours, provided the rate of the leak does not increase.

An aquarium full of water should not be moved, or it will be seriously strained by the internal water pressure.

New sealers are legion, notably the 'rubber coat' that lies over, and hence cures the gaps. And the fabulous bonding silicone used in aeroplane construction that bonds glass to glass with a purchase or grip of a mere centimetre or so. Used everywhere, this has removed the necessity of wide angle frame supports. All-glass tanks are now common.

13

Water Enemies and Diseases
(Tropical and Coldwater Fish)

THE great danger when catching live foods for a pond or aquarium, or when procuring plants from untried sources, is that water-enemies will be introduced as well; these are small aquatic insects which can kill or harm baby fish and in at least two instances even medium-sized adult fish. The main water-enemies are the Water Tigers, Dragon Fly larvae, and Hydra.

The Water Tiger is a long and thin insect, shaped rather like a caterpillar, and has two vicious pincers with which it can hold its victim and through which it can suck its blood. It grows to 4cm. or more, but probably its most dangerous size is half-grown as it is then difficult to detect. A good swimmer, it can tackle and kill fish twice its own size.

The Dragon Fly Larva is similar to the Water Tiger except that it does not swim much but lies in wait for its prey. The victims are merely held by the pincers and are then destroyed by its hard mouth, which can do amazing damage even through the sturdy scale protection of quite big fish.

Hydra is different from the two described above, being very much smaller and capable of harming only fry. Its presence is betrayed by a group or bunch of thread-like streamers or hairs hanging in the water; these are the tentacles. Each hydra is roughly 2cm. long, having about half a dozen tentacles spread out like a star fish. Since it invariably seems to multiply rapidly, ways have had to be found to remove the vast numbers other than by emptying and cleaning the pond or aquarium.

The aquarium can be purified by raising the temperature to 38°C. for twenty to thirty minutes (no fish being present, of course), or by introducing Blue or Leeri Gourami fish, which will eat the hydra when forced to do so by sheer hunger – so they should not be fed by the aquarist in the meantime. These allies can be obtained from your dealer and are best in the normal home tank. Some English water snails (limia stagnalis) will also eat hydra, but they have the bad habit of eating plants as well.

One more way of eliminating hydra is to black out the tank entirely – tops, sides and bottom – leaving only a 5cm. × 5cm. gap on the side facing the light. Within a few hours all the hydra in the dark tank will have gathered on the 5cm. × 5cm. opening and can then easily be wiped off with a sponge.

For the pond, one-quarter of a grain of potassium permanganate can be added for each $4\frac{1}{2}$ litres of water; if no fry are present at the time the dose can be doubled. This should be left for two or three days and the water then gradually changed until half to two-thirds of the original has been replaced. The fish need not be removed. Another alternative remedy for the hydra-infected pond is ammonium sulphate added to the water at the rate of one teaspoonful to every 45 litres; this also will destroy the enemies but not the fish.

These three then, Water Tiger, Dragon Fly Larvae, and Hydra, are the main water-enemies, but the list is by no means exhausted. Some 'foreign' creatures are, however, quite harmless and are rapidly eaten by such fish as the Barbs, who seem to enjoy the change of diet.

The obvious moral is not to introduce these pests in the first place! This cannot be guaranteed, of course, but the practised eye of an expert can afford fairly sure protection as he will take every care to screen his live foods and plants before selling them to the public. The same remarks apply forcefully to the diseases described below; indeed they serve to emphasize why the isolation of fish, stressed in Chapter 1, is so very necessary.

The diseases are divided into two groups: Tropical and Coldwater, not because there is a cut-and-dried distinction between them, but because they apply more often to the class of fish under which they are listed. The suggested cures and symptoms apply to both classes. Obviously all nets, instruments, etc., should be sterilized after use to prevent the spread of infection from the isolation tank.

Starting with the Tropicals:
White Spot.

These parasites look like tiny white dots on (not in) the fish, usually showing first on the tail or behind the eyes. After a normal cycle of some 10 days the spot falls off, breaks into fragments, each of which actively seeks a host fish and must succeed in 24–48 hours, or die. This is the vulnerable period when cures can be effective. Left untreated, one single spot can soon multiply to wipe out the entire tank.

Originally there were only two main kinds of this spot. With atomic radiation of our planet daily increasing there are now a full seven different mutations – mostly virulent.

Originally, white spot disease was contracted by a chill, or other weakening; now it is indigenous in the wild waters of Africa, Asia, South America, and has begun to spread in Europe and in North America. The very act of taking a fish from one tank and putting it in another of identical water and identical temperature is sufficient to bring out the disease. A sobering thought.

The old cures were to raise the tank temperature to 29°C. or even 35°C.; but African and Asian waters are hotter than that. Try see-sawing the temperature daily from 21°C. to 32°C. to 21°C. This causes some aquarists to shudder in dismay; my earlier books would have done so too, but it can 'work' on the principle of weakening the micro-organism (protective cyst notwithstanding) quicker than the fish.

Malachute green ($\frac{1}{4}$ grain per $4\frac{1}{2}$ litres) is the basis for many 'instant' cures now sold; very strong, so the dose has to be ultra-carefully measured. There is no need to raise the tank temperature – a point to note.

More standard medicines coupled with a 6°C. temperature raise include: *Methylene Blue*, you should make the water light to Oxford Blue, but not darker than that, and leave for 10–16 days; *Quinine hydrochloride* (1 gram for 90 litres), dose for 5–10 days; and *Aureomycin* ($\frac{1}{16}$ grain per $4\frac{1}{2}$ litres).

In every case, the tank water should be changed, perhaps in two doses, after cure.

Dirt does not help; darkness, or dim light, does. Aeration and live foods (lightly administered) are advised.

Flukes is an irritant disease caused by a parasite, and provokes the usual reaction to irritation, viz. the fish rubs itself against the rocks or sides of the aquarium and darts at high speed only to stop suddenly. Like White Spot, this disease is contagious.

It should be treated by placing the affected fish in a shallow dish containing one drop of glacial acetic acid to each 28 grammes of water (of the same temperature as that in the tank) and leaving it there for a *few seconds*, say fifteen or twenty. If this is unsuccessful, the same treatment should not be given until the fish has rested for at least thirty-six hours; during this period it could be fed with live food.

An alternative is to add one gramme weight of Methylene Blue to $4\frac{1}{2}$ litres of water, making the colour a dark blue, and to leave the fish in this solution for fifteen to twenty minutes.

As flukes can cause difficulty in breathing, the use of gentle aeration is helpful.

Shimmies. In this, the fish sways rapidly from side to side and yet does not move forward even though it appears to be 'swimming'. These shakings are easily recognized.

The cause is either a chill, or unsuitable aquarium water which has become poisoned by excess urine, by harmful nitrites (as distinct from nitrates), toxic substances transferred into the water by air or by hand, or by plain old-fashioned dirt.

The cure is to raise the temperature to 31°C., for seven to twelve days, and to change the water with 'old' water – that is water that has been standing for thirty-six or forty-eight hours. Feed well on live foods in the meantime. Aerate.

Dropsy and Wasting Disease
Dropsy causes the scales of the fish to stick out in a most repulsive, bloated fashion. Mild cases, which are strongly suspected of being a form of indigestion, are sometimes cured by a four-hour bath in a solution of two level teaspoons of Epsom Salts per $4\frac{1}{2}$ litres of water (of the same temperature as that in the tank). The cause of Dropsy is thought to be a worm in the intestines, but what makes it attack particular fish is not known.

Dropsy can be cured by withdrawing the exudate a few millimetres before the anus with a hypodermic syringe; by feeding the fish with foods pre-soaked in medicines of triple strength, or by direct dosages of oxytetracycline or of chloro-mycetin (30 to 90 milligrammes per $4\frac{1}{2}$ litres in 3 doses). Contagious if the exudate escapes into the water.

Wasting Disease is what the name implies. The fish begins to waste away, starting from the tail, and becomes miserably thin, finally dying. Various theories are advanced in explanation: the fish is old; the general tank conditions are poor (Chapter 5); or the fish was forced-bred (Chapter 1). All these can be true in part, but none fully explains this puzzling disease.

The above diseases attack tropicals more frequently than they do coldwater fish, for whom the main ones are as follows:

FUNGUS

A white cotton-wool-like smudge appears on parts of the fish, and is easily recognized. The cause is very often bad conditions, such as overcrowding, poor feeding, or prolonged low temperature, etc., as detailed in Chapter 5. Bruises and knocks can sometimes also begin the ailment, which is highly contagious. Obviously, the suspected bad conditions must first be remedied to prevent a recurrence or a spread of the disease.

The cure is one that applies very frequently to coldwater fish, and one that can perhaps be used even where the complaint cannot be diagnosed and an 'anything is better than nothing' policy is felt advisable. This salt treatment is accordingly described in detail:

SALT TREATMENT
Rock salt, or, failing that, cooking salt, should be used; table salt is not safe as it contains chemicals to keep it dry and powdery.

There are two methods of application, somewhat conflicting so both are described here. The first is the older, conventional one; the second is the newer.

METHOD NO. ONE FOR SALT TREATMENT
Place the fish in 'old' water of the same temperature as the tank and add two level teaspoons of rock salt per $4\frac{1}{2}$ litres and leave for a day.

During the next day slowly build up the dose to four level

71

teaspoons, and finally on the third day to six level teaspoons of rock salt per 4½ litres of water.

By now the fish should be cured and 'old' water of the same temperature can be added until the salt content has been eliminated. Should the cure need to be prolonged beyond three days, a new saline solution should be made as the other will have tended to become stale.

METHOD NO. TWO FOR SALT TREATMENT

This is a four-day cure, by giving the fish four baths, one a day, in a saline solution freshly made each day; the fish is to be left in the bath for four hours daily before being transferred back into fresh water. Great care *must* be taken that there is no difference in the water temperatures when the fish is transferred from the salt to the fresh and vice versa. This point is of the utmost importance, otherwise the fish will be harmed, not helped, by these salt baths. The fish should be excited as little as possible while being caught in a net to be transferred from one water to the other.

The strength of the saline solution is:

1st day: two heaped teaspoons of rock or cooking salt per 4½ litres.

2nd day: four measures.

3rd day: four measures.

4th day: two measures.

Feed the fish well each time on its return to fresh water; keep it in dim light during treatment.

ALTERNATIVE TREATMENTS

New drugs like Phenoxethol are the basis for many patented medicines sold to cure fungus. The following do-it-yourself ones could be tried:

Swab with iodine, or mercurochrome, or merthiolate, *all diluted 1000 times:* i.e. 1 cc. in a litre of water; alternatively add these in 2 or 3 doses to the tank (changing the water after cure).

For more stubborn cases: Potassium dichromate (2½ grains per 4½ litres), Phenoxethol (dilute 1 cc. per litre, and then give 10 to 40 drops per 4½ litres); Malachute green (¼ grain per

4½ litres); Terramycin (50–200 milligrammes per 4½ litres, in several stages), or Sulphamerazine sodium (4 grains per 4½ litres).

Always administer medicines in several stages, in case your tank water over-reacts; keep the tank in dim light; aerate it; feed the fish with live foods; allow no dirt; change the tank water at the finish of the treatment.

A much more drastic treatment, which can be tried in 'kill or cure' attempts, is a solution of ten drops of ammonia in 4½ litres of water, leaving the fish in it for not more than five minutes; if, however, the fish begins to show signs of acute distress and starts losing its balance and turning on its side, it should be removed at once.

TAIL ROT AND FIN CONGESTION

These are two separate diseases, both caused by bad conditions (Chapter 5) or by a sharp fall of temperature. The symptoms are blood-red streaks or veins appearing on the fins or tails, which will drop and crumple.

The cure is the fungus treatment already described.

A more drastic cure is to hold the fish gently but firmly in a damp cloth and to cut off the affected parts, afterwards disinfecting the wound with a pink solution of potassium permanganate. Alternatively, the diseased parts can be burned off with a 50 per cent solution of hydrogen peroxide; once the affected parts have been dipped in this solution they will fall away about forty-eight hours after the fish has been returned to the aquarium.

There remain three main diseases to which both tropicals and cold-water fish are equally prone:

CONSTIPATION

This is indicated by long excreta threads hanging from the fish and by a general bloated appearance of the body.

Cure is to leave the fish four hours in a solution of Epsom Salts (one heaped teaspoon to 4½ litres of water), or feed with live Daphnia.

BLADDER TROUBLE

Fish have a swim bladder filled with a gas and regulated so that they can rest in comfort at any angle and at any depth. If this gas pressure is not exactly right, the fish will stay at the top and have difficulty in reaching the bottom of the tank; or, conversely, will stay at the bottom and have to make strenuous efforts to rise – only to sink again when exhausted.

Mild attacks are sometimes caused by indigestion, and the constipation treatment mentioned above might help. Relief can also be given by placing the fish in shallow water of a very slightly higher temperature, e.g. rather less than 1 °C. Although uncomfortable, the fish is not in pain and there is no need to destroy it, particularly as the disease is not contagious.

Swim bladder trouble is very often the result of a sharp temperature change, particularly if the fish has been taken from one container and put in another without the temperature of the two waters being equalized beforehand. Sometimes a cure can be effected by giving the fish a four-hour bath in a mixture of sodium acid phosphate and of household ammonia, strength one flat teaspoon of sodium acid phosphate and five drops of household ammonia to fifty-four litres of water. But the mixture must be freshly made. Obviously, too, the mixture must be the same temperature as the aquarium water.

POP EYES, BRUISES, GENERAL PROTUBERANCES

When the eyes stick out and swell, or swellings appear on the body as a result of bruises, etc., a certain amount of hit-or-miss treatment can be employed. If these symptoms are the result of internal disorders they are virtually incurable as so little is known about them. When, however, they are the results of external blows or cuts, the affected parts could be gently wiped with cotton wool soaked in a strong solution of boracic acid (at the rate of three heaped teaspoons per $4\frac{1}{2}$ litres of water). Alternatively a mixture of one drop of iodine and ten drops of glycerine could be used. The fish should then be left alone for a week to await results.

When the protuberances are caused by parasites lodging under the skin, the fish can be held in a damp cloth and have the affected spots touched with one drop of a purple solution with one drop of 2 per cent Mercurochrome. Potassium permanganate at this strength will burn the skin of the fish and should be applied only to the exact spot of the protuberance; if this is not large or severe, the Mercurochrome treatment should be enough by itself.

A subsequent bath for four hours in a salt solution of two heaped teaspoons of rock or cooking salt per 4½ litres of water is beneficial.

Alternatively, a bath for five minutes in a solution of one teaspoon of T.C.P. disinfectant to each half litre of water will kill most lice without harming the fish; if the fish starts to heel over on to its side, however, it should be returned at once to fresh water of the same temperature.

A new disease, temporarily called *Velvet* for want of a better name, is linked to those described. The fish is covered with fungus or threads of rootlike tentacular growth and dies unless treated promptly. It can be immersed for twenty minutes in a solution of one gram of Methylene Blue, of best medical quality strength, per 4½ litres of water, or it can be given the full salt treatment described previously in this chapter, when recovery should follow.

A similar disease is Gill Worms, which may be treated by putting the sick fish in a solution of 4½ litres of water and twenty drops of commercial formalin, increasing the strength in half an hour to forty drops per 4½ litres. Then remove the fish to a salt water solution, of the same temperature (strength one tablespoon of cooking salt per 4½ litres). After four to six hours replace with fresh water of the same temperature, either by siphoning or with a jug, until the salt solution has been eliminated. Repeat the whole process each day for three days.

Yet another method is helpful: a bath, for twelve *seconds* only, in water to which has been added Dettol at the rate of four teaspoons to each 4½ litres. Repeat after eight to twelve days if necessary.

CONCLUSION

Whether a fish is sick or just 'feeling off-colour', the following points will help both coldwater and tropical fish:

A change of water and of surroundings, by transference to another tank, often acts as a tonic more especially if the new tank has green water. As always, care must be taken to equalize temperatures before transference.

The addition of aeration, or, in the case of coldwater especially, of very gently running water, has the same effect as taking a city man to the seaside or for a short holiday.

Dim light, shallow water, and live food are all three a great help. The chemicals mentioned (potassium permanganate, salt, etc.) should first be dissolved in a little water before being used; they should never be dropped in as solids in fish water and allowed to dissolve there, because the act of dissolution sets up very strong local chemical reactions and liberates strong gases.

Finally, a plea for restraint must be made. The difference between 'leave well alone' and 'too late to cure' is finely shaded and it is a question of some judgement when or whether to begin a cure for a suspected disease. After all, there still is a strong moral in the story of the healthy man who began to read medical books; studying the various symptoms he convinced himself he suffered from each and every disease (except housemaids' knee) until he had to visit his doctor for a course of reassurance!

New Medicines

These improve daily, especially as the medical profession is now becoming involved in the aquarium trade, and sophisticated advances are common. Your specialist dealer should be abreast of these; otherwise the 'standard' cures already described should help – you could experiment by uniting the medicines in 'cocktail' admixtures for stubborn cases.

14

You, The Customer

WHERE else can you get a pet that is tame; that learns to know you personally; that will come when you call; that will so easily spawn for you and present you with extra pets, newly born; that will let you go away all day or even for days on end without bothering about feeding, without wondering if it will make a noise, without worrying if it will cause a mess, without needing to be taken out for exercise, or even to be given attention at any particular fixed times; a pet that has such lively colours and shapes; that looks so attractive in its miniature water garden; that intrigues and delights your guests; that furnishes a gently-soothing and absorbingly-relaxing point of interest; a pet that will do all that and yet need only five minutes' attention PER WEEK.

The fact that your pets need so little attention does not mean that they can get along without any at all! So please do be considerate. If things go wrong it may be the fault of the dealer, it may be the fault of the fish, or it may be your own.

The dealer should do his very best to provide only healthy fish, but how can he possibly *guarantee* that a living thing will not fall sick. After all, you take great care of yourself, provide yourself with the best practicable living conditions and food, but could *you* guarantee that you would never fall ill or need a doctor?

In the vast majority of cases the customer–dealer relationship is a very harmonious and close one, but there is the exception (fortunately very rare) of the selfish customer who always demands that his work be done NOW, oblivious of what others may need, and who blindly assumes that the dealer has nothing else to do but to serve HIM. In his own eyes, too, this customer can do no wrong; if there is a fault then it must be someone else's – never HIS.

The aquarium is very simple to keep, is very beautiful and

77

does not need a lot of attention. If yours goes wrong then there is a reason and that reason can be found and eliminated if you will work with your specialist dealer.

15
Ponds

THE following points will make a big difference to the pleasure of the owner and to the health of the fish:

1. Build the pond strongly so that it will not crack after hard frosts and ice; minimum wall thickness is 30cm. at base tapering to 13cm. at top. Corners and base should be reinforced.

2. *Depth*. Either by sloping the floor or by building it in ledges, varying depths should be provided from 25cm.–125cm. At 125cm. the fish are pretty well protected from outside enemies and from changes of temperature, either excessive heat or cold. A further protection is to build at this depth a sort of 'home', i.e. a box open at one side into which they can retire in case of marauders – birds, cats or small boys. The shallow parts will be enjoyed by the fish on warm sunny days and should be furnished with marginal plants.

3. *Location*. Normal sunshine is most desirable but not to excess; all-the-day-long exposure to the sun is almost certain to turn the water green. On the other hand, a lack of shelter from east winds is not helpful. Dead leaves foul the water so that direct overhanging trees ought to be avoided. Excessive dirt and mud can be kept out of the pond if its edges are above the immediate ground level.

4. Facilities for emptying and refilling the pond either through an overflow pipe or by means of a siphon to some lower level will be a great asset.

TREATMENT OF NEW PONDS

The cement of newly built ponds contains chemicals harmful to fish, and the best plan is not to try and isolate them from the water by coating the cement with water glass or with one of the many patent protections, but to remove the harmful chemicals altogether.

A simple way is to fill the pond with water, to add enough potassium permanganate to turn the water in one day from pink to red to dark red and then finally to purple. After being thus soaked in dark purple for five to seven days, the pond can be thoroughly washed out, refilled, and will be ready for fish after the water has been standing for ten more days. New patent treatments for 'instant' neutralization of lime are also available and are recommended.

PLANTS

There are four main types of pond plants: border or marginal, that grow in 8cm.–23cm. of water; submerged oxygenators; lilies; and floating plants.

Instead of covering the base of the pond with earth, loam or even sand – all of which will tend to cloud the water – experience indicates that a better method is to plant bunches in porous boxes or trays of wood or in flower pots and then immerse; they can be readily removed in case of need. Heavy loam, held in place by peat or by sand, is the best planting medium, and it can be renewed from time to time, depending on the relative size of the roots and of the box.

There are many of these plants available, of lilies alone there are some two hundred varieties, but the more popular ones are as follows; any specialist dealer will stock them:

Marginal. Often with flower on which the insects will alight to lay their eggs and help provide natural foods for the fish.

> Forget-me-nots
> Arrowheads
> Iris
> Marsh Marigold
> Buttercups
> Mint
> Rushes and Reeds

Submerged Oxygenators help to keep the water sweet. They also provide a nursery where the eggs can hatch and the fry can grow in some degree of safety, and then feed on natural foods, such as infusoria, larva, louse, shrimps, and daphnia.

Too many plants will choke a pond but fairly plentiful and thick bunches should be provided leaving the fish enough room to swim freely.

The main submerged oxygenators are:

The Elodeas
Water Crowfoot
Starwort
Fontinalis
Hornwort
Myriophyllum

Liles. The large spreading leaves of the lily provide admirable shade for the fish and greatly encourage the development of natural insect life. Liles are particular regarding the depth of water and their leaves will curl up if this is wrong or they are planted too near each other. Of the huge number of varieties available the Laydeckeri group favour 30cm.–40cm. water depth, and the Odorata 45cm.–60cm. depth. The use of special baskets is recommended for planting. Good sunlight is essential if they are to flower and flourish. *Floating Plants,* i.e. those that are not rooted in anything but draw their nourishment either from the atmosphere or from the water; they are excellent for providing shade where needed. Naturally, since they float, there is no planting required in this case, all that is necessary is to put them in the water, preferably not upside down.

POND FISH

As has already been stressed these are in a different category from coldwater aquarium fish, being in the main quicker consumers of oxygen dissolved in the water; they are bigger, for one thing, growing to over 45cm. in length, and living for twenty to thirty years *and more.* They are often fast swimmers into the bargain so that they burn up more energy and therefore need more oxygen. Although they have been kept in coldwater tanks it cannot be too strongly emphasized that it is not fair to the fish, which suffer a protracted agony of stunted growth and slow suffocation.

Goldfish, Silver Rudd, Golden Orfe, Nymphs, Comets, even Fantails are all perfectly happy in ponds. The addition of scavengers – fish that grub around cleaning up the bottom is advisable; notably the Prussian and the Golden Carps, the Tench, and the Catfish. Moderate numbers of snails and mussels can be used.

River fish such as Pike or Perch are killers and must not be introduced; nor should Minnows, since they prefer fast moving waters and are often carriers of disease.

Feeding. In summer-time, particularly if the weather is good, the fish will find natural food in a well-planted pond; even so they could be given a small pinch of prepared food per fish twice a week. If, however, deliberate breeding is being attempted or the colour development of a fish is being forced we refer the reader to Chapter 9 for instructions. From mid-September to mid-November serious attempts should be made purposely to fatten up the fish, so as to build up surplus fat and energy the better to enable them to survive the winter. Once the water temperature falls below 10°C. the fish become sluggish and do not eat; this winter hibernation lasts through until the warm weather of spring and no food should be given during the whole of this period.

The fattening-up process can be done by supplying a daily feed of worms, obtainable from a dealer or from compost heaps in the garden; in addition a lump of cold porridge the size of a gooseberry once a day per fish is advisable.

Of course, the dates stated in this chapter are approximate, being governed by the state of the weather and by the location and depth of the pond.

PREPARING FOR THE WINTER

There are two main dangers both equally important especially in the case of the smaller ponds.
1. *Freezing.* Providing the pond is 125cm. deep in one part at least this battle is practically won so far as the normal British climate is concerned. When the top of the pond is

coated with ice it is a good plan to leave this unbroken except for two or four holes through which the air can circulate; then some 5cm. of water can be siphoned off leaving a protective air cushion in addition to the protective ice layer and so minimizing the danger of any more of the pond water freezing. Snow 'blacks out' a pond and must be swept off the ice. The holes can best be made by standing a can of hot water on the ice until it melts; breaking with a hammer might crack the sides of the pond. A piece of sacking over the holes might prevent re-freezing.

2. *Foul Water*. This danger is often overlooked but it is very real. During the warm months the pond water content of gases and of minerals gradually increases, due to the decomposition of fish droppings, decaying leaves, and other such natural causes, until a high concentration is reached. In a frozen pond with its limited air openings this high concentration can cause the water to go foul. Thus the following precautions are necessary in late November:

(a) Cut back the growing submerged plants to within 15cm. of the bottom, removing all excess.

(b) Carefully remove as many dead leaves and as much foreign matter as is possible.

(c) Change one-third to half the water gradually over twenty-four to thirty-six hours.

If the frozen pond later seems to be going foul in spite of these precautions then the risk of gradually changing a quarter to a third of the water in winter will have to be run.

SPRING

This is the time fish may die as a result of the rigours of the winter, but there is little that can be done as the main remedies lie in attention during the previous November onwards to the points outlined above.

At this time, too, there is a particular danger of the water going green if the days happen to be bright; as the reader already knows, light promotes the growth of green microscopic life, algae, and since the plants have not yet started to grow and to compete for the even smaller living organisms that serve

83

both algae and plants as food, the development of green algae is unhindered. Live Daphnia can be introduced into the pond and will soon eat up the algae thus clearing the water; when the fish start eating as the spring warmth raises the pond water temperature they will eat the Daphnia in their turn.

WATER CLOUDINESS IN PONDS

In the case of ponds, the remarks on water cloudiness in Chapter 5 apply, but in a slightly different form.

White cloudiness is very rare indeed and can more or less be ignored. Brown cloudiness is also less prevalent unless the pond is too shallow to allow floating matter to settle quickly, or unless large amounts of dirt, mud, dead leaves, and so forth are at the bottom and are being stirred up by fish, particularly such fish as the carp or tench which love to burrow and grub along the bottom sediment.

Green cloudiness, however, is a common complaint in the bright days of summer. The only preventative is to try to shade the pond surface – floating plants, or lilies with spreading leaves are helpful. Also, strongly-growing submerged plants hinder the development of algae. There are different forms of algae, of course, but for practical purposes they can be treated as the one described in Chapter 5, except for the pernicious form known as 'blanket-weed' – that is, the long blue-green strips and even webs that entwine and suffocate plants.

The only cure for this horrible weed is to clean out the pond thoroughly and to disinfect it by adding permanganate of potash to the pond water until a dark red colour is attained, for twelve to thirty-six hours; at this strength blanket-weed is killed, but so are plants and fish – which will need to be removed. The plants should be washed gently in a pink solution of permanganate in order to disinfect them, but the most affected ones should be thrown away as the reappearance of blanket-weed might well be encouraged if even the slightest amount of the weed is left on the plants.

GENERAL FACTS

The gallon capacity of a pond can be determined by multiplying in feet the length by the width by the depth by $6\frac{1}{4}$. The capacity in litres is the length by the depth by the width in centimetres divided by 1000.

For a circular pond multiply in feet the diameter by the diameter by the depth by 4·9 to get the number of gallons. For litres multiply half the diameter by half the diameter by the depth (all in centimetres) by 3·14, and divide by 1000.

The number of fish that can be kept is one body inch of fish per square foot of water surface. Thus a 10 ft. by 3 ft. pond (30 sq. ft.) will hold ten fish 3 ins. long, not counting finnage.

Measuring metrically, you can say that 1cm. of fish needs 365 sq. cm. of water surface area. Thus a pond of 3 metres by 1 metre could hold around ten fish each 8cm. long.

Spawning, rearing and water enemies have been dealt with elsewhere.

Fountain pumps have the same effect as aeration detailed in the appropriate chapter.

Rocks should not be used for the simple reason that they cannot easily be seen; their purpose is decorative, so as they are not visible, why use them? A rockery round the edge is quite a different matter.

Pool heaters that prevent winter freezing are now readily available and can be a great boon.

Rigid ponds, made of plastic compounds, can be plonked literally on your sitting-room carpet to make a most pleasing indoor pond. Increasingly popular are the indoor ponds raised on decorative stands (often incorporating flowers/speciality lighting) to bring the pond up to standing or to sitting level – so that you can talk to the fish, tickle them, cup them in your hand (immersed in the water), and generally tame these lovable pets.

Add a small fountain and/or a waterfall cascade and you also have the therapeutic soothing sound of gently falling water – marvellous for relaxation.

Add a heating unit; combine it with exotic plants, partly submerged, partly surface, partly growing up into your room; have the full range of tropical fish available; and you'll wonder why you never had it before.

16

Coldwater Fish for the Aquarium

THE FANTAIL

Mᴀxɪᴍᴜᴍ life thirteen years. This fish will breed after surviving one winter, but it is better to be developed for another year or so before breeding. It is still lively at the age of ten years and is a hardy pet which takes most foods and can live out of doors throughout the year.

At 16°C. to 21°C. it spawns readily, the eggs hatching in four days. Four spawnings a season (April to September) is ample. Born a dark greenish brown, the best specimens develop in four to eight months into a warm gold. Our illustration clearly shows the best type of egg-shaped body and finnage, together with their relative proportions.

THE LIONHEAD

The body is that of a Veiltail, with the finnage of a Fantail. The pimply growth gives it its distinctive appearance and name

and takes four to six years to develop. A rare fish. Has no dorsal fin. Likes aeration to help in its breathing, which is rather laborious due to its tremendous growth on the head. Can easily be killed by the water becoming foul or otherwise running out of oxygen.

THE ORANDA

Very similar to the Lionhead except that the growth of its mane is not so pronounced; a fact compensated for by a distinctive dorsal fin. Hardy.

THE SHUBUNKIN

The hardiest of all coldwater aquarium fish. Like the Fantail it can also live in ponds. Average life fourteen years. Our illustration shows an excellent specimen, both as regards body shape and finnage. The covering scales should be quite transparent, showing a beautiful assortment of mottled colours; blue should predominate over smudges of red, brown, yellow and violet with a peppering of black flecks. Breeding is similar to the Fantail.

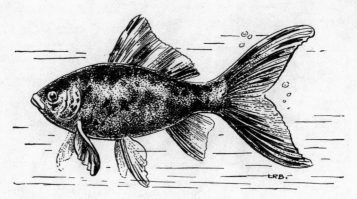

THE CALICO VARIETIES

Similar in colouring to the above, but with bodies resembling those of the Fantails. Great favourites.

TELESCOPIC-EYED BLACK MOOR

Jet black, double-tailed and telescopic-eyed – those are its characteristics. Very short-sighted. A fish which requires careful feeding, including algae, but is otherwise hardy and adaptable. A good plan is to drop the food in the same place each time, calling the fish by tapping gently on the glass. Dislikes cold and should not be below 10°C., preferring 18–21°C. Good light, but not bright sunlight is appreciated.

THE TELESCOPIC-EYED VARIETIES

These include many exotic and somewhat rare specimens now being flown in from the Far East; notably Bubble-Eyes and Celestial-Eyes. Lovely creatures.

THE VEILTAIL

Our illustration clearly shows the rounded body, as distinct from the egg-shaped one of the Fantail, and the different finnage especially in the entire absence of a fork in the caudal fins. Average life twelve years. Not really hardy enough for ponds. Its beauty entitles it to a place in the aquarium. Most Veiltails available are similar in colour to Fantails, although a truly prized specimen – a rare phenomenon – should be coloured like the Shubunkin.

Needs carefully balanced foods. Very difficult to breed as the number of throwbacks is frustratingly high; similar breeding methods to those for the Fantail can be used except that the temperatures can be up to $2\frac{1}{2}$°C. higher. This fish needs plenty of water and space. It is sensitive to sudden temperature variation.

17

Tropical Fish-Livebearers

As is now well known there are fish that do not lay eggs but give direct birth to live baby fish, miniature creatures about ½cm. long, but fully formed and able to swim almost at once. The eggs are fertilized and developed inside the mother; during the period of gestation they are kept folded in half, head to tail. The length of the gestation depends on the aquarium conditions, but principally on the temperature, which should not be too low.

In livebearers the sexes are easily distinguished. The male anal fin quickly develops into a pointed instrument known as the gonopodium; normally carried at rest parallel to the body and pointing backwards, it is brought right forward for use when the act of fertilization is imminent. The female anal fin is rounded.

The males are promiscuous and have no interest whatsoever in caring for their young. Curiously enough, a single fertilization can result in four separate spawnings by the female without any further contact, the spawnings each being separated by as many days (usually thirty or so) as the original period of gestation.

After fertilization the female gradually begins to swell, and her gravid spot, which is close to the vent, becomes darker and darker, and more and more intense in colour as the time for delivery approaches, when anything from half a dozen to fifty or even a hundred young are born. These are just over ½cm. or more in length, and can swim more or less at once, otherwise they would not escape the cannibalistic tendencies of their mother, who should be separated from them by breeding traps or some other device. The simplest device is to use massed plants, including floating Riccia; the fry have a natural instinct to swim towards the light and the protective thickets should be arranged accordingly. Well-fed adults do not make serious attempts to seek out the young.

Most of these viviparous fry are already past the infusoria stage at birth and, accordingly, at warm temperatures of 24–27°C. develop rapidly *provided* they have plenty of room. Frequent feeding, even four to eight times daily, is advisable; the surplus food is eaten by snails or by corydoras fish specially introduced to scavenge.

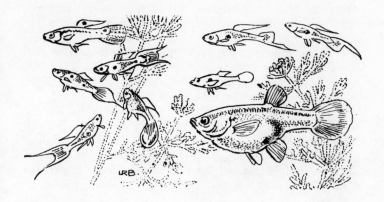

THE GUPPY

The Guppy, scientific name *Lebistes reticulatus*, is by far the most famous and the most easily bred of all the livebearers. Maximum length is 6cm. for the female and just over 3cm. for the male, not including the tail.

No two males are alike although selective breeding can so fix major characteristics that there are numerous recognized sub-divisions such as the Lyre-Tail, Sword-Tail, etc., apart from the distinctive Golden Guppy.

The Guppy really has everything: lovely colourings (in the male only), hardy, active, playful, but extremely peaceful; stands temperatures from 16–38°C., eats anything, even lives in foul water and seldom falls sick. Our illustration shows various types of coloured males, and one gravid female with her dark 'gravid' spot clearly visible.

At 22–27°C. the period of gestation is only four weeks, but below temperatures of 20°C. it is prolonged to nearly twelve weeks. At 26°C. the fry, which can number from six to fifty, will grow so rapidly that they will be ripe for reproduction after as little as six weeks! Frequent feeding is almost essential. After two years a Guppy is definitely old.

THE MOLLY

These are of four main kinds, all having a body shape not unlike a female Swordtail, and all vegetarian by preference.

Molliensia sphenops is the most often encountered. Growing up to 10cm. in length, it is born silvery, becomes speckled with black and in rare cases finishes a pitch velvet black; usually the body remains spangled with an attractive blue-gold sheen. The males sometimes have an orange-tipped tail.

Terribly greedy, it eats practically all the time and is liable to overfeed; it loves green algae, or failing that boiled spinach. Bright sunny location, clean tank, old water and temperatures of 24–27°C. suit it well. A lively fish, it is peaceful to the point of being easily frightened, and is therefore liable to nervous diseases. It should not be netted or disturbed more than is necessary.

A gravid female becomes flustered and agitated in a confined breeding trap; in any case, she should never be disturbed when the delivery time of her young is less than two weeks away. A bang of a room door or sudden movements will frighten her, so that shade and privacy are practically essential.

Seasonal breeders, the aquarist should aim to have a virgin female some nine months old in breeding condition in April. At 24–27°C. her first spawning will be ready in eight weeks, and the subsequent three spawnings approximately thirty to thirty-five day intervals after this first one. Then the female should be rested until next year. The young can number anything from six to forty, and are nearly 1¼cm. long at birth.

The best fish do not develop their sex characteristics before nine months. First the anal fin ceases to grow, then it loses its rounded trailing edge and becomes narrow and pointed. It shrinks, becomes more narrow still, shows signs of detachment and finally becomes pointed. Then the gonopodium starts to grow. The chest of the male is far more square and wide.

The Molly is different from other livebearers in regard to the degree of nervousness and of the importance played by the seasons in breeding.

The other main types of Molly are:

Mollienisia latipinna, famed for its magnificent sail-fin and for the pitch velvet black of its body. Beautiful specimens are rare. The first ray of the dorsal starts in front of the highest point of the back; in the Sphenops it starts at the back of this highest point.

Perma-Black Molly. A comparatively new strain. It is born black and stays black; the trouble is that it never grows large.

Liberty Molly, whose body remains an uninteresting silver but whose dorsal is tricoloured, by way of compensation.

All these, and the others not mentioned, are being cross bred to give lovely new varieties.

THE PLATY

The Platy, former scientific name *Platypoecilus maculatus,* is another favourite livebearer, and has contributed to a greater and more interesting assortment of hybrids than almost any

93

other fish. The male length is 4cm. and the female 6cm. The main recognized sub-divisions are as follows:

Black Platy, so called because of the dominating bank of black that runs lengthwise from head to tail. The fringes of the body are tinged with green or yellow, and the fins are often white.

Blue Platy, of various shades, but with a blue-green gloss predominating.

Golden Platy, with a rich yellow body, often has a red dorsal fin.

Moon Platy, whose distinctive feature is a crescent-shaped half moon in the tail.

Red Platy, beautifully blood-red, is not quite as hardy as the others. The colour becomes deeper with age.

Wagtail Platy, whose tail can almost be imagined to wag the body. The dorsal and ventral fins are well developed too; the fin colouring is usually black.

From the above half-dozen kinds there have been very numerous crosses; it will be remembered that they are all Platys and will interbreed without any heed to colour or markings.

They have a distinct preference for variety in their diet, but will take anything, not forgetting algae or boiled spinach. A temperature of 23°C. is ideal. Most types of water will do, but a mature, clean tank is probably best.

In thickly planted tanks which include floating plants the parents are not too liable to eat the young, especailly if plenty of other food is available. Breeding temperature is 23–27°C.

THE SWORDTAIL

The Swordtail, former scientific name *Xiphophorus, hellerii*, has a maximum length (excluding the male tail sword) of 8cm.

This Green Swordtail, and its more famous derivative the Red Swordtail, is a great jumper; otherwise it conforms to the livebearer type as described for the Platy. The males have a tendency to fight among themselves especially if insufficient females are present. It is very liable to develop 'shimmies' after even a single chilling, and should be kept at 23–27°C.

The best males do not grow their swords until they are some

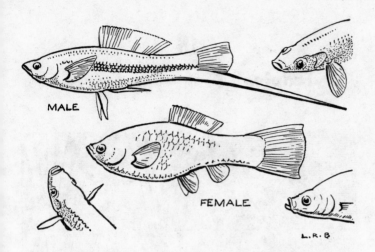

MALE

FEMALE

L.R.B

eight to ten months old and reach about 5cm. in length; once the sword has started to appear the fish does not grow much more. Likes plenty of light and can spawn up to two hundred young.

So much interbreeding between the livebearers has taken place, to give so many new strains (like the Hi-fins) that the former scientific names are no longer valid.

18
Tropical Fish – Egg-layers

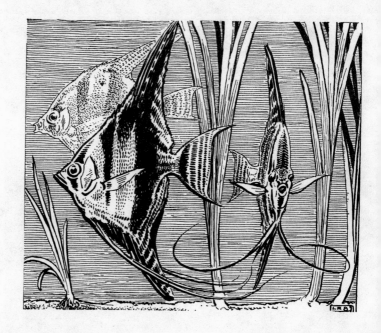

ANGEL FISH

Scientific names, *Pterophyllum eimekei*, and *Pterophyllum scalare*. Maximum length 13cm.

'The queen of the aquarium' – certainly its distinctive shape, its quietly effective black markings on the silver body, and its dignified movement, especially in a group, earn it the adjective 'royal'.

Happiest when in the company of other Angel Fish, this lovely creature should not be kept alone. An asset to any community tank, the Angel is inclined to be a little shy and might need to be fed separately; indeed, it is a little finicky in its food preference and is liable to go on hunger strikes. Live foods, above all Daphnia, are well received. Normal temperatures of 23–25°C. are best.

The real secret of keeping Angels is in the Soft DH 4 aquarium water. If this is not suitable the fish does not thrive, and positively refuses to breed. Even if it has bred the eggs prove infertile and do not hatch.

The prospective parents should be allowed to choose themselves by putting a group of fish together and allowing them to pair off, otherwise they will not harmonize. The preliminary courting is more like quarrelling in its violence, and has been known to end in death unless the fish were separated for a while before being reintroduced. Because harmony is essential the vexed question of determining the sex can better be left to the fish themselves, although two female Angels have been known to pair off and to produce infertile eggs!

The following points will help to sex an adult fish. The female tube for depositing eggs is more rounded than the male and tends to point backwards; strong light shone through the fish shows the female intestine to be more rounded and less flat at the top; the space between the ventral fin (the 'feelers') and the anal fin is greater and is straighter in the female although the anal fin leaves the body at a sharper angle in the case of the male; the lower jaw of the male sticks out very slightly more; the general impression in a side view of the male frame is that he is slightly more rounded in appearance than his mate.

The breeding tank should be crystal clear and free of dirt. Two hours' direct sunshine coupled with some shade is ideal. Strong-leafed plants such as sagittaria, amazon swords, or cryptocorynes should be plentifully available to take the adhesive eggs, although ample swimming room is required. Temperature 24°C. Increased aeration, a very slight increase in acidity using acid sodium phosphate, a 1°C. lowering of the temperature will often induce the previously harmonized and conditioned pair to spawn.

As the eggs are laid in small quantities and at fairly spaced intervals the eggs on the plant leaves should be removed to water of exactly the same type and temperature. 8–10cm. depth is enough. Gentle aeration is extremely helpful. If this constant removal of the eggs proves too costly in plants, strips of slate 5cm. wide could be used instead, especially as these will not rot (like the leaves) during the comparatively long hatching period. Infertile eggs should be removed as they tend to swamp the others.

At 26–27°C. the eggs hatch in about forty-eight hours, the fry being free swimming in five to six days, although not reaching recognizable shape for some four weeks. The fry need plenty of oxygen, and aeration helps, so does soft water.

ALSO AVAILABLE

Lace Angels, Veil-Tail Angels, Black Angels, Malayan Angels, Glass Angels, Marble Angels, Blushing Angels, Bicolom Angels, and many others.

BARB – ROSY

Scientific name *Barbus conchonius*. Maximum length 9cm.

There are very many varieties of Barbs obtainable nowadays and they are lively and attractive additions to the community tank.

The Rosy Barb, like all its cousins, is hardy, playful to the point of being boisterous, always hungry and willing to eat practically any type of food, long lived (up to eight years), thriving best in old water and in bright locations. Temperature preference 23–26°C.

The male dorsal fin is black at its leading edge, while that of the female is almost colourless. Both have a black spot on the tail. At breeding condition the female is greenish gold and full bodied; her mate is a bright rosy red.

Spawning is fairly easy and lasts about two hours. Temperature 27°C. Plenty of space for the driving of the female by the male is required, as are thickets of cabomba and myriophyllum to catch the practically non-adhesive eggs, and act as some means of protection for the eggs – as described in the breeding of Zebras. The water can be 20–30cm. deep.

The eggs hatch in two days at 27°C. and the fry are hardy; in fact the main problem is to find enough room for the possible three hundred arrivals!

OTHER BARBS

There are more than thirty types available, including many firm favourites:

CHERRY. Peaceful, almost shy, lovely colours during breeding condition, small.

OLEGELEPIS. Also small and peaceful with varied checkered markings.

TICTO. Similar to the Rosy but with a more striking top fin, and with a luminous spot on the tail.

AURILIUS. Rather longer and thinner than the others, growing to 10cm. and displaying pronounced black markings.

HEXAZONA. Long, sleek, colourful and well behaved.

GELIUS. Dwarf variety, and comparatively rare.

BARB – TIGER

Scientific name *Barbus tetrazona* (formerly *Barbus sumatranus*). Maximum length 5cm.

Another of the more popular Barbs, it has a colourful red and black appearance, especially at temperatures above 24°C. Extremely lively, smaller specimens are better for the community tank.

The red in the ventral fins is more pronounced in the male; the female is fuller bodied.

Temperament and spawning are as described for the Rosy Barb. Needs a lively playmate, and is best kept in pairs.

BEACON FISH

Scientific name *Hemmigramus ocellifer*, sometimes known as Head-and-Tail light fish, from its two luminous spots. Grows to nearly 5cm. in length.

It is peaceful but lively. Sex characteristics are usual for its type (it is a characin) in that at breeding condition the female is fuller in the body and is very liable to hen-peck. In our illustration the small white fleck in the anal fin of the upper fish denotes the male. There is another specie of this fish where the male has two white flecks near the luminous point on his tail.

The fish have a wide temperature tolerance but prefer 23–24°C. and will breed best at 23–26°C. As usual, spawning is best done by conditioning the pair separately, introducing the female first into the nuptial tank in the afternoon and slightly scared male later that evening. Next morning spawning should commence, and will last up to four to five hours. If the male is being too hen-pecked the operations should be postponed till he is in better condition. Mature water, sufficient for a depth of 10–15cm., and the bushy clumps of myriophyllum and cabomba for the semi-adhesive eggs, which hatch in twenty-four hours at 26–28°C., should be provided. The addition of floating plants will help. The bottom of the breeding tank should be clear, and not be littered with pebbles or small stones.

MOENKHAUSIA OLIGOLEPIS

Included here because it looks similar to the Beacon although it belongs to a different group. Its luminous spots are more definitive. Decorative and peaceful. An albino variation is also available.

HEMMIGRAMMUS PULCHER

Again similar to look at; its tail luminous spot is very strongly outlined.

BLACK WIDOW

Scientific name *Gymnocorymbus ternaetzi*; it grows to 5cm. but is at its best at 3–4cm.; afterwards it becomes pale and loses the wonderful black markings from which it gets its name.

The caudal fin is transparent and hardly noticeable; the dorsal and anal fins and the rear half of the body are black; and the silver front half of the body is marked by three black bands. Our illustration does not quite bring out the peculiar disc-like shape.

It is a lively fish, but quite peaceful. Sex differences are not apparent, except that the female at breeding condition is fuller in body and considerably more assertive than the male. If a strong light is shone through the body the female intestine will be seen to be more rounded, the male one slightly angular.

Tolerating a wide temperature range, it breeds at 26–27°C. Love play begins with female driving the male from end to end of the tank until he is goaded into action. In spawning the male repeatedly brushes the ventral of the female, tilting slightly as he touches her; the movements are rapid, but the eggs can be seen to fall. Some 150 eggs are laid in batches of a dozen or so.

At 27°C. the adhesive eggs hatch in twelve to twenty-four hours, and the fry become free swimming in four days.

OTHER ROUND-SHAPED FISH

Included here because of their similarity in shape to the Black Widow.

DISCUS. Almost completely circular, with wonderful markings when grown to its full size of 30cm. diameter. Expensive, but highly prized.

SCATAFAGUS. Also striking and with the approximate shape of the Discus. Nicely marked (there are several varieties) and medium priced. Likes salt and has to be acclimatized (by the dealer) to fresh water before sale. Unacclimatized specimens are offered for sale cheaply but are almost literally a dead loss!

HATCHETS. Both the Silver Winged and the Marble types are shaped like an inverted half-moon with a flattened back. Top swimmers. Hardy.

CATFISH – GLASS

Scientific name, *Kryptopterus bicirrhus*. Maximum length 10cm.

One of the strangest of all aquarium fish, it is almost completely transparent, and our illustration endeavours to show that apart from the yolk sac and the bone structure very little else is visible!

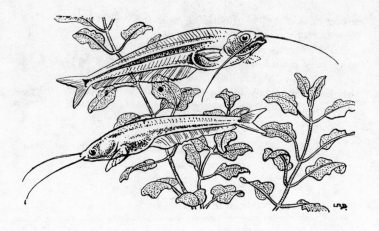

With advancing age the glass-like appearance yellows and it tends to become opaque.

A peaceful fish, it is very short-sighted and therefore has difficulty in catching such foods as live daphnia. Tubifex worms are traced by means of its long feelers which are stretched right forward when it is on the hunt.

Prefers old water and a fair amount of mulm at the bottom of a thickly planted tank of cryptocorynes and amazon swords.

Has a disconcerting habit of staying in one place usually a few inches below water surface, and 'shivering'; rippling from side to side almost as though it had the disease called 'shimmies'. Temperature 25–28°C. Dislikes light. Quite hardy. Likes to shelter under broad leaves.

BUTTERFLY FISH

From Africa. Most unusual. Is a top swimmer and jumper and is a most attractive addition to the community tank. Likes 27–31°C., and feeds from above.

In passing you might like to know that over four hundred and eighty varieties of tropical fish are currently sold in the better specialist shops; all these fish being peaceable with a good temperature and food tolerance.

It is naturally not possible to list all in this book, so you can well afford to experiment with new fish – on the advice of your dealer.

CATFISH – SUCKING

Scientific name *Otocinclus affinis*. Maximum length 5cm.

Another peculiar fish, the large suction mouth is useful in holding the fish in chosen positions, or it can be used as a miniature vacuum cleaner to remove food and algae from glass sides, rocks, plants, leaves, etc. When in an upside down or vertical position it uses its strong pectoral and ventrals to hang on.

Peaceful, hardy and very industrious, it likes well-planted tanks, old water, not too much mulm and sunny locations to help develop algae. Temperature preferred is 24–27°C. It hates bare empty tanks with no rocks or other furnishings on which it can perch. It takes normal foods, but is a little inclined to overfeed on Tubifex. Aeration welcomed.

It breeds in a similar way to Corydoras Aneus.

CORYDORAS

There are a number of aquarium species of these delightful fish. Peaceful and industrious, they spend their time grubbing about the floor of the aquarium eating left-overs of food, and fully earning their title of scavengers. Their rather sleepy lazy attitude during the day should not be misunderstood, as they are largely nocturnal. In fact they are very hard workers. At frequent intervals they will dart up to the air surface to take in a drop of atmospheric air, but they are not full fledged labyrinth breathers, although they can live in quite foul waters. As young fry they do not appear to develop this ability under four to six weeks, and are very sensitive to lack of oxygen in the aquarium or to dust on the water surface. If prevented from reaching free air, above water, they will drown.

Some of the more popular Corydoras are listed:

Aneus. Sometimes called the Green Catfish; prefers lower temperatures than normal, e.g. 21–23°C., breeds at 22–24°C., eggs hatch in three to four days.

Arcuatus, or Arched Catfish, after the dark arching line running from eye to tail, so pronounced on its pale body.

Julii, or Leopard Catfish, from the very beautiful markings all over its body, dorsal fin, and tail. Has three horizontal stripes on each side, and a black spot on top of its dorsal fin.

Melanistius. Is very similar to the Julii except that it does not

106

have the horizontal side stripes and dorsal spot, but two dark vertical smudges on the body, one through the eye and the other from the forward base of the dorsal fin.

Our illustration is of *C. Paleatus*, one of the most plentiful of the 'armoured catfish'. While bringing out the barbels and heavy scaling, justice has not been done to the blue-black dappled markings found on the body especially under the dorsal fin. In common with the others it grows to 6–8cm. in length.

Breeding is easy. The female is more plump and full bodied, her dorsal and ventral fins are more rounded, and her belly and the first ray of her pectoral fins are slightly tinged with colour.

Love play starts with the male repeatedly swimming over the female caressing her with his barbels and ends with them locked together, the male lying on the floor heeled right over with the female resting her chest on his. On separation the female carries the eggs in her ventral fins to the chosen plant, or aquarium glass which she mouths thoroughly before pressing the adhesive eggs on to the surface. The spawning may last for an hour or two before the two parents ignore each other, and the eggs. Just as a precaution, however, the adults should be removed.

The spawning tank should be 15–23cm. deep, with clean sand, some strong-leafed plants like sagittaria or amazon sword plants with mature water, and a temperature of 23–24°C. The eggs hatch in seventy-two to ninety-six hours at 23°C.

EELS

Scientific name *Acanthopthalmus semicinctus*. Length under 8cm. (Other kinds grow much larger, to the detriment of the aquarium.)

In common with the Corydoras these are also noted as scavengers. There are several kinds of which one only is described here.

Our illustration shows the pale belly, the barbels, the dorsal and the pectoral fins. The ventral fins are half-way along the body length, often at the seventh set of markings counting from the tail, i.e. two markings past the dorsal.

Above water vegetation to give streaked light and twigs on the top 3cm. of water are essential for breeding. The male persistently swims over the female and caresses her with his barbels. It is believed to like fairly high temperatures, 25–29°C., and to appreciate aeration. As with the Corydoras, it is nocturnal. It will eat most foods and is quite hardy. Likes twigs to perch on, or gaps to hide in, even when adult.

EX-RAYS

Scientific name *Pristella riddlei*. Length only 4–4½cm.

Its popularity is long established as a peaceful and lively foil for more brightly coloured fish. The stark contrast of its black markings on a white body is completed by a faintly pink tail.

The dark mark on the anal fin of the female goes right across; on the male it appears as a patch with a clear strip at both ends. At breeding condition the female is somewhat more full bodied.

Bred in mature water of 18cm. depth, the fish likes a tank planted with bushy myriophyllum and cabomba, especially towards the lighted end; temperature should be 23–25°C., at which the eggs will hatch in a day. During spawnings, the parents indulge in energetic driving, and finally end up side by side, quivering violently, fertilizing the adhesive eggs which are laid on the vegetation.

FLAME FISH

Scientific name, *Hyphessobrycon flammeus*. Maximum length 4cm.

A beautiful little fish, not flamboyant in colour but whose red flush is warm, especially on the tail half of the body. peaceful and hardy, it has a preference for a bright, well-painted tank, free from dirt. It has a very wide temperature range and an average life of four years.

The anal fin in the male is pointed and is fitted with a small hook on the end; the hook is invisible to the eye, but often gets caught in the fine meshing of a net. The outline of the female is not so straight as that of her partner, in fact it is more nearly concave. A strong light shone through the fish shows the female intestines to be more rounded than the slightly angular ones of the male.

24–27°C. is a good breeding temperature. Plenty of cabomba, myriophyllum, or other such plants, old water, slight aeration and two males to one female make up the ideal. The male drives the female vigorously before they take up a side by side position, trembling violently, and releasing the eggs in batches of a dozen every few minutes. A hundred eggs constitute a reasonable spawning. Obviously the parents should be removed before they can eat the eggs.

At 24–27°C. these will hatch in some sixty hours and the fry become free swimming in about four days.

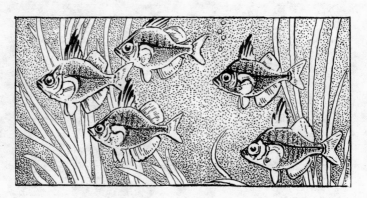

GLASS FISH

Scientific name, *Ambassis lala*. Maximum length 4cm.

As indicated by its name, it has a glass-like transparency showing the intestines, swim bladder, backbone, and even the small bones; an outside light shone through the side of the fish gives a most pleasing effect. There is a strong tendency to go yellow and opaque with age.

Normal temperature should be 23–26°C. and very old or even brackish water is preferred.

Sex differences are more apparent at breeding condition

110

with the blue rimming on the dorsal and the anal fin being stronger on the male. In our illustration the top left-hand fish is the male, with rounded intestines; the female in the bottom left-hand corner has her intestines hollow at the top.

When conditioned to breeding stage a change to neutral or even very slightly acid water will often stimulate the fish into action, particularly if the temperature is raised to 26–28°C.

The tank should be 13cm. deep and planted with cabomba and myriophyllum to catch the adhesive eggs; these hatch in a day at 27–28°C. The spawning actions are spread over two to four days; the eggs and fry are not always eaten by the parents but they should be removed as a precaution.

The fry are minute in size and finding small enough food is the main difficulty in rearing them. Infusoria made with cow dung is best. Fortunately the babies grow very fast especially in a large tank, say 80cm. long by 20cm. high by 30cm. wide, and will soon take normal foods.

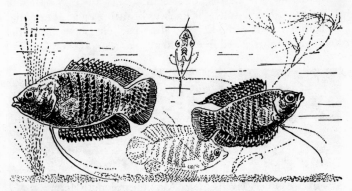

GOURAMI – DWARF

Scientific name, *Colisa lalia*. Maximum length 5cm.

The colours of the male are truly fascinating; if the illustration can be imagined to have a delicate blue background on to which bright red markings have been thickly woven to give the appearance almost of red stripes with dozens and dozens of red dots peppered over the tail, some idea of its delicate beauty is obtained. The female is much less attractive being more of

111

an olive green with markings of an indefinite orange. Naturally, at breeding condition the colours of both fish are intensified. The male feelers have more colour in them at all times.

Definitely on the shy side, the Dwarf Gourami needs plenty of plants and hiding-places. It does not flourish in deep water; it likes high temperatures round 26–27°C., water that is old, but very slightly acid, soft and some sunlight. Very fond of greenery it is almost a vegetarian and should always have some algae; it will take normal foods which are not too large for its small mouth. It is somewhat prone to catch the disease known as dropsy if crowded and without protective clefts in the rocks that it can shelter in.

As a labyrinth breather it conforms to the habits of its cousins the Lace Gourami and the Siamese Fighting Fish with two slight differences: the breeding temperature should be 27–28°C., and myriophyllum should be present to be incorporated in the bubble nest. Sometimes the female helps in the construction. The nest is about 8cm. across, the eggs hatching in thirty-six hours at 27–29°C. A tight-fitting cover is essential to help keep off draughts and dust particles for at least the first two months. Need free air to gulp as soon as they develop.

GOURAMI – LACE

Scientific name, *Trichogaster leeri*. Maximum length 10cm.

The great popularity of this fish has given it a variety of

names: Lace Gourami, Pearl Gourami, Leeri Gourami or Mosaic Gourami. Its appearance is beautiful rather than flamboyant, richer in markings than in hues; with a fine pearly lace-work on the silver background, threaded throughout by an irregular black line from the mouth to the tail, this lovely fish has bold outstanding finnage and magnificent feelers.

With a wide temperature tolerance it flourishes at 23–25°C., and has a preference for old water. A small eater it should be fed fairly often, say three times a day. Has the virtue of eating Hydra when it is hungry. At least one good thicket of plants to serve as a hiding-place is essential, as it is not a boisterous fish and likes to retire for privacy and peace.

A labyrinth breather, it builds bubble nests in common with all its type. This peculiar breeding process has been fully described in the section on Siamese Fighting Fish.

The Lace Gourami simply will not breed if it does not like its surroundings. Old, neutral water pH 7·0, temperature of 27°C., a fairly large tank say 60cm. by 30cm. by 20cm. high, with some mulm at the bottom and plenty of plants especially cryptocorynes, Amazon Swords, Aponogeton, and Vallisneria and also some floating plants – all these combined should induce it to spawn.

The male is not as rough with the female as some other labyrinth breathers, but she should be removed after the eggs are laid; he can be left with the nest, and even with the fry for three to four days if desired.

Some 250 eggs are laid in a bubble nest measuring 9cm. across and ¾ to 1½cm. deep and they hatch in twenty-four hours at 27°C. A tight cover is essential to keep off dust and draughts until the fry are two months old.

The sex differences are apparent only at breeding condition: the female being fuller, the male having a bright red breast and rosy feelers. Incidentally he never quite loses these colours later on if he is in good health. The first few rays of the anal fin are thicker and more pointed in an adult male, and his dorsal fin is longer.

HARLEQUIN

Scientific name, *Rasbora heteromorpha*. Maximum length 4cm.

A delightful fish that has always been a favourite of the community aquarium. A striking black triangle dominates the rear half of the body, the fringes of which are tinged with red.

In the male the golden line running the upper length of the triangle is broader and more pronounced than in the female. The body of the female is more plump. Sometimes in the male there is a tendency for the bottom of the vertical side of the triangle to point forwards.

Peaceful and hardy, the Harlequin is at home in any temperature from 21–32°C., but prefers 25–28°C. It will eat almost any type of food. Usually swims about 15cm. from the water surface, likes new water, slightly acid, and benefits from aeration, and softened to DH 6–8.

Breeding is not too difficult, and the following may help: heavy clumps of strong-growing cryptocorynes at one end of the tank with the sand sloping high up from the back right down low to the front; new water that has been standing in strong light, preferably sunlight, for two days; pH 6·2 obtained by the use of rotting leaves rather than by sodium acid phosphate; dimmed light; gently dripping water at the planted end; temperature 25–28°C.; clean tank free from sediment; a very small amount of iron in the water say 1·5 parts per million; two males to one female, and DH 6–8.

Spawning first starts when the female swims upside down under selected leaves, rubbing herself against them, the male being in excited attendance. When he joins her under the leaf in a trembling embrace, the adhesive eggs are produced, fertilized, and are stuck on to the leaf. The action lasts for about ninety minutes, with rests, and several leaves are used. As has already been suggested the tank should be clean as algae covering the plants prevents the eggs adhering properly and fallen ones are soon eaten. Parents should be removed as soon as is practical. Fifty eggs is quite a satisfactory result; at 28°C. they hatch in one day.

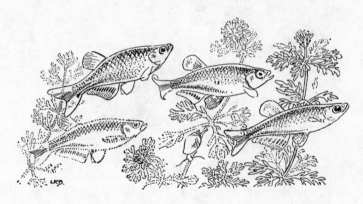

PEARL DANIO

Scientific name, *Brachydanio albolineatus*. Maximum length 6cm.

The wonderful mother-of-pearl hues shine brightest when the fish is seen by a reflected, not a top, light, and the arresting colours of the anal fin are then seen to best advantage. Gleams of purple, red and gold, and the flashing row of pearl dots brighten the make-up of this fish.

Peaceful, extremely lively, it is similar in habits and in breeding to its cousin the Zebra. The ways of sex differentiation are the same.

The best breeding temperature is 31°C. and it is the female that begins the courtship until the males are sufficiently roused to assume control. Better results are obtained by using a smaller tank say 45cm. by 25cm. by 15cm. high, and by having two males to one female, whereby a higher proportion of fertilization is ensured for the eggs. Some 250 in number, they hatch in two to three days at 31°C.

It is essential that the water surface of the breeding and rearing tanks be kept free of dust particles and film.

SIAMESE FIGHTING FISH

Scientific name, *Betta splendens*. Maximum length 6cm.

Perhaps the most famous of all the aquarium fish, the male can be breath-taking in his beauty – greens, blues, reds, lavenders, purples – all hues to delight. Two males fight on sight; in fact, the national sport in Siam is to match these finny stalwarts against each other, and to place heavy bets, especially where pedigree champions are involved. During the fight, which can last several hours, fins are ruthlessly ripped and even blood can be drawn.

The aquarist can safely keep one in his tank, as the male disdains to attack any other fish as being an unworthy opponent. Rather, he tends to be lazy and sulky, lurking in odd corners, and displaying his beautiful colours on somewhat rare occasions. He has a wide temperature range but prefers 23–25°C. His life span is only three years.

When the fish get to 3cm. in size the sexes can be identified. The females are peaceful, are drab in colour, and have shorter, more rounded fins; the males are exactly the opposite in each point.

Because they fight at even this early stage they have to be kept in separate jars. Fortunately these jars need not be large because the Siamese fighters are labyrinth breathers and therefore have an auxiliary breathing apparatus for taking oxygen direct from the air, as well as from the water by using their gills in the normal way; deprived of this, they die.

The breeding actions are also unusual. The male fish builds a floating nest constructed of air bubbles supported by odd bits of plants, twigs, etc. The bubbles are blown by the male and are slightly coated with saliva so that they do not burst too easily; the average size of the nest is some 8cm. by 5cm. by just over ½cm. The female may help in this construction but it is more likely to be done by her larger and more powerful mate. A good breeding temperature is 26°C. and the addition of floating topweed and of good light is helpful.

Incidentally, the male who is ready to breed is liable to kill a female who is not. Choosing a pair, therefore, requires considerable care; this can be done, for example, by keeping them separated by a sheet of glass until they both show signs of interest, and even then allowing them to be together for only brief periods at first. At all times, too, there should be thickets of plants or other hiding-places where the female can retire for rest or protection.

The nest built, the male drives the female under it, almost wraps his body around her, turns her upside down and practically squeezes the eggs out of her. During this embrace the two fish slowly sink to the bottom. The eggs are fertilized as they are laid. This breeding action may go on for as long as an hour, and two or three hundred eggs, or even more, may be carefully gathered and wrapped in a separate bubble before being put into the nest.

When the female begins to retire to her hiding-places more and more she should be removed. It is usually safe to leave the male behind for two days to tend the fragile nest, and industriously to replace any burst bubbles.

At a temperature of 26–28°C. the eggs hatch in two days. Old water is preferred.

One final word of warning. The young fry do not develop their auxiliary breathing apparatus for three to four weeks and are peculiarly susceptible to draughts or to dust on the water surface; a close-fitting top cover is therefore advisable.

TETRA – GLOW LIGHT

Scientific name is not known for certain but is currently accepted as *Hyphessobrycon gracilis*. Maximum length 4cm.

Beautiful is the only word to describe the shining eyes and the phosphorescent, warm-glowing streak running the length of the body. No black and white illustration can do it justice.

It is best kept in groups of four or more. Peaceful and hardy, it is not finicky about food, although being a small eater prefers frequent meals. It likes a high oxygen and a low carbon-dioxide content in its water, which should not be too old and which can profitably be aerated. The aquarium should be clean, and kept at 23–24°C.

The breeding tank should be most carefully sterilized, be in dim light, be about 13–18cm. deep and be kept at 27°C. Aeration helps. Spawning action is energetic, usually at water

118

surface, and is over in thirty to forty minutes; the fish momentarily locking fins and rolling over on to their sides. Eggs are fertilized during the embrace, and a dozen or so are produced at a time. They are semi-adhesive and clumps of myriophyllum or cabomba make ideal spawning ground; about thirty-six hours are enough to hatch the eggs.

This fish is subject to the 'Neon Tetra Disease', a description of which is in that section, and should be kept in darkness for the first five days.

CARDINAL – TETRA

A comparative newcomer that has finally displaced the Neon Tetra as the most beautiful of them all. Rather shy, it grows to four times the size of the Neon *without* losing any of the phosphorescence or any lessening of the brilliance of its colouring which is almost exactly the same as that of a Neon, but with a peculiar extra 'lightness' of shade. There really are no words to describe these two fish – you will have to see them for yourself. The red line extends right into the tail, the Neon's stops short at the peduncle.

NEON – TETRA

Scientific name, *Hyphessobrycon innesi*. Maximum length 4cm.

Surely all hobbyists have heard of this most dazzling

aquarium fish. Our illustration simply does not do it justice, as no illustration, not even one in colour, could do that. Running lengthwise is a brilliant blue-green streak and immediately underneath another one of a bright red. Both lines seem luminous, and the effect is startling. Hardy and peaceful, the Neon will eat most foods, although its mouth is small, too small sometimes even to take daphnia.

It prefers temperatures of 22–24°C. and likes shade and privacy. The only sure way to tell the sexes is to wait for two adults of a group to pair off, the female being more full bodied.

Breeding the Neon has long been a challenge but the difficulties are now overcome. Firstly the parents must be healthy and free of the 'Neon Tetra' disease; of this there are no external or visible marks although the muscle tissues are sometimes slightly whitish. Infested fish lose weight and persistently lay infertile eggs. The disease is uncurable; a parasite, protozoan, infects the intestines and the spore formation. Thus the presence of even one 'carrier fish' (i.e. one that is infected, but not virulently) can poison the water so that eggs do not hatch. Very great numbers of fish are so infected although they appear quite healthy and live for a long time. Aureomycin or methelyne blue can help in light doses sufficient just to tinge the water.

The main difficulty, then, is to get healthy parents. Furthermore they must harmonize, and have been brought up separately to breeding condition. Soft water, three days old, 12–70cm. deep, pH 7·0 to 7·2, temperature 22–23°C., clumps of myriophyllum, and absolute cleanliness make up the breeding tank. *Absolute* cleanliness is vital, and everything will have to be most thoroughly scalded and sterilized; in fact there are some breeders that just do not believe this can be sufficiently well done and insist on a bare, all-glass tank, with one propped-up flat stone to whose underneath the fry can later cling. Very dim lighting is also important, and as soon as the normal spawning has taken place the hatching aquarium should be kept in continuous darkness for five to six days. Furthermore, the water depth can be reduced to 6cm. Both these two unusual precautions seem to increase the proportion of fertile eggs. Hatching the eggs, not laying them, is the real trouble; some 200 can be laid and are practically non-adhesive.

The fry are small, even when compared with other types of fry, and the greatest care in feeding is required. At 23–26°C. the eggs should hatch in twenty-four hours and the alevin become free swimming in four days. Remember, though, that continuous darkness is essential at this stage and that no direct light must be admitted to the tank, so that there is no means of examining the fry before the sixth day after spawning. Thereafter the light can be gradually returned to normal, but strong lights are to be avoided.

WHITE CLOUD MOUNTAIN MINNOW

Scientific name, *Tanichthys albonubes*. Maximum length 4cm.

When young it looks just like a Neon Tetra with the luminous bright green streak, but this gradually fades as adult size is reached and becomes greenish-yellow. As a compensation the red colour develops in the fins. Incidentally it is in these fins that is seen most clearly the difference between the two distinct strains that are said to exist.

Peaceful and hardy, the fish has an amazing temperature range from 7°C. to some 32°C., but should normally be kept round 22°C. In common with most small-mouthed fish it prefers frequent feeding, say three times daily, and likes soft, new water of pH 6·8.

The male being more colourful and slimmer bodied than the female, also has a longer dorsal. The breeding habits are the same as that for the Zebra, with the non-adhesive eggs hatching in seventy-two hours at 22°C. Because the spawning action lasts for a week or so the best results are probably obtained by separating the adults from the eggs by means of glass rods, wire mesh or any other such device. Unlike the Zebra, these fish are not so prone to eat the eggs.

ZEBRA FISH

Scientific name, *Brachydanio rerio*. Maximum length 4cm.

A delightful fish, fast swimming, playful and active but not mischievous, looks best in schools when the blue-black horizontal stripes on the pale background flash in the light. The background fluctuates through white to silver or even to yellow depending on the lighting and on the surroundings; the darker the bottom of the aquarium, the darker the colours on the fish.

With a very wide temperature range it does best in 23–24°C. Has a comparatively short life span of three years and high temperatures tend to shorten this even more. Keeps near the surface and prefers to eat there; it will take almost any kind of food.

122

The sexes are not easy to identify. The female is more full-bodied, and is more arched than the male between the back of the head and the dorsal fin. At breeding condition the white body spots on the male colour into brownish pink. In our illustration the top fish is the male.

In spawning the main problem is to prevent the eggs being eaten. There are special breeding traps that allow the eggs to fall through but which prevent the parents following, or a layer of coarse pebbles and a breeding depth of 10cm. of water can be used, the eggs falling fast and being protected by the crevices forced by the pebbles. Brought up to condition, separately, the female should first be introduced into the breeding tank, the male the same evening, and the spawning can be expected next morning at first light if the temperature is raised from 22–23°C. to 22° C. At first the female chases the male, but the roles are soon reversed.

About 100 eggs are given out in excited bursts, and are fertilized by the male, the action taking place right close to the top of the water, almost out of it at times. If he is in poor condition or if the eggs have been too scattered a high proportion of infertile ones can result, the rest hatching in two to three days at 26°C. The parents should be removed after spawning. Neutral water of pH 7·0, not too old, is best. Groups of plants in which the males can corner the females and urge them to lay, are advisable.

CONVERSION FACTORS

One Gallon	=	4·546 Litres
One lb.	=	0·4536 Kilogramme
One Inch	=	2·54 Centimetres

To work out Centigrade temperatures in Fahrenheit, divide by five, multiply by nine, and add 32. The answer will be the number of degrees Fahrenheit.

for example: 45°C. = 113°F.

$$\left(\frac{45}{5} \times \frac{9}{1} \right) + 32 = 113°F.$$

Index

125